ENDLESS LIFE

poems of the mystics

ENDLESS LIFE

poems of the mystics

Adaptations and Translations by

SCOTT CAIRNS

PARACLETE PRESS
BREWSTER, MASSACHUSETTS

2014 First Printing This Edition
Endless Life: Poems of the Mystics

Copyright © 2007 by Scott Cairns

ISBN: 978-1-55725-520-2

Originally published in hardcover in 2007 as *Love's Immensity: Mystics on the Endless Life*

The Paraclete Press name and logo (dove on cross) are trademarks of Paraclete Press, Inc.

The Library of Congress has catalogued the hardcover edition as follows:

Cairns, Scott.
  Love's immensity : mystics on the endless life / adaptations and translations by Scott Cairns.
    p. cm.
  ISBN 978-1-55725-525-9
  I. Title.
PS3553.A3943L68 2007
811'.54—dc22   2007005036

10 9 8 7 6 5 4 3 2 1

Published by Paraclete Press
Brewster, Massachusetts
www.paracletepress.com

Printed in the United States of America

Contents

Preface   xi

Prologue   xv
   "Late Request"
   from *The Cloud of Unknowing*

Saint Paul the Apostle   3
   "Beyond Knowing"   3
   "Love's Body"   4
Saint Irenaeus   5
   "Capable Flesh"   5
   "The Human Person"   6
Saint Melito of Sardis   8
   "Pascha, Our Passing over into Life"   8
   "Christ Speaks"   9
   "How It Was"   9
Origen of Alexandria   11
   "Of Us All"   11
   "All in All"   12
Saint Athanasios   13
   "The Invisible Seen"   13
   "The Death of Death"   14
   "His Image Recovered"   15
   "As a Good Teacher"   16
   "Scant Offering"   16
Saint Ephraim of Syria   17
   "The Prayer of Saint Ephraim"   17
   "Due Praise"   18
   "Fountains of Blessing"   20
   "The Living Bread"   21
   "The Messenger Who Came"   22
   "What Bides Waiting"   23

Saint Syncletica of Alexandria   25
  "Sayings"   25
Saint Makarios of Egypt   28
  "Awaiting Prayer"   28
  "The Human Soul"   29
  "A Union"   30
Saint Macrina the Younger   31
  "Prayers"   31
Saint Basil the Great   34
  "Illumination"   34
  "A Prayer"   35
Saint Gregory Nazianzos   37
  "The Shepherd"   37
  "The Soul's Permanence"   38
  "Spiritual Being"   38
Saint Gregory of Nyssa   39
  "His Death Our Life"   39
  "Soul's Eternal Rapture"   40
  "Allegory of the Soul"   41
Mother Theodora of Egypt   42
  "Sayings"   42
Saint Augustine of Hippo   44
  "A Speculation"   44
  "The Beatific Vision"   45
  "Soul's Purpose"   46
  "Prayer"   47
  "The Eighth Day"   48
Evagrios of Pontos   49
  "Effusions on Prayer"   49
Saint Denys the Areopagite   61
  "As Beauty Bids"   61
  "Beckoning Beauty"   62
  "As No Other Being"   63
  "Paradoxical Love in Revelation"   64
  "No Separation"   65

Saint Dorotheos of Gaza   66
"Where We Are"   66
"Visitation"   67
Saint John of the Ladder   69
"Prayer"   69
"Purpose and Order"   70
"If You Would Prevail"   71
Saint Isaac of Nineveh   74
"Love's Purpose"   74
"The Measure of His Mercy"   75
"The Merciful Heart"   75
"Mystery Beyond the Words"   77
"Gehenna, Its Duration"   78
"Awaiting Us at Last"   79
Saint Francis of Assisi   80
"Mercy"   80
"The Reach to Speak His Name"   81
"His Blessings and His Praise"   82
Saint Clare of Assisi   83
"The Depth of His Touch"   83
"The One Thing Necessary"   84
"Paradox and Promise"   85
Bléssed Angela of Foligno   86
"His Entry and Delight"   86
"A Vision"   87
"Divine Light"   87
"His Blazing Embrace"   88
"The Darkness"   89
"His Doing"   90
Saint Nicephorus the Hesychast   91
"Reunion"   91
"New Knowledge"   92
Mechthild of Magdeburg   93
"Love's Four Things"   93
"God's Splendor Reflected"   94
"How We Become Like God"   95

Gertrude of Helfta   96
  "Prayer and Pleading"   96
  "Of Humility and Worthiness"   97
  "At Vespers"   98
Meister Eckhart   99
  "The Prayer of a Heart Detached"   99
  "Unburdened"   100
  "Beyond Sorrows"   101
  "The One Image"   101
Saint Gregory Palamás   102
  "Uncreated Light"   102
  "To the Summit of Tabor"   104
  "Effort and Study"   104
Richard Rolle of Hampole   105
  "God's Love"   105
  "Invitation to the God"   106
  "Love's Effect"   107
Julian of Norwich   108
  "His Suffering Love"   108
  "The God Alone"   110
  "His Comfort"   110
Walter Hilton   113
  "The Soul, His Spouse"   113
  "What the Light Reveals"   114
  "Knowledge unto Knowledge, Evermore"   115
Nicholas of Cusa   116
  "Knowing Nothing"   116
  "Within the Cloud"   117
  "His Mercy"   118
Saint Catherine of Siena   119
  "Waking Desire"   119
  "A Revelation"   120
  "Inebriated Soul in Love"   121

Saint Catherine of Genoa   122
   "Agapi"   122
   "In the Crucible"   123
   "Provisional Matters"   124
Saint Nil Sorsky   125
   "What Affections Avail"   125
   "The Gift of Tears"   126
   "Sayings"   126
Saint John of the Cross   128
   "Dark Night"   128
   "Love's Living Flame"   129
   "Ecstatic Stanzas"   131
Saint Nicodemos of the Holy Mountain   133
   "Noetic Vision"   133
   "The Mind's Home within the Heart"   135
   "A Plea"   136
Saint Thérèse of Lisieux   137
   "Eternal Canticle"   137
   "Attend"   138
   "The Flower"   139
   "The Holy Face"   140

Epilogue   142
   "The Words" from *The Zohar*

Preface

This collection is a mere taste of the bountiful feast that awaits any who would pursue a life of faith and prayer, equipped with both the holy Scriptures and the holy tradition that surrounds them.

Having done time—the first forty or so years of my life—snug among the *sola scriptura* crowd, I spent a good bit of that time reinventing the prayer-wheel. That wouldn't have been such a bad thing, I suppose, if any of my poor prototypes had turned out like anything approaching the well-grounded, efficacious, and frankly quite beautiful construction that preceded me and mine.

This book is but an introduction to some of the rich and enriching tradition that has always (perhaps until the twentieth Century) and everywhere (except, perhaps, large sections of North America) been understood as an expedient accompaniment *to* and illumination *of* the Scriptures, and has long been understood to be of great assistance to the spiritual life. It is, after all, only relatively recently that the terms *tradition* and *Scripture* have been mistaken for separate, and perhaps even antagonistic authorities.

It is good to note that even Martin Luther—the father of our cranky phrase *sola scriptura*—was himself utterly well-equipped *with* and assisted *by* a rich and enriching communion with the tradition expressed by the fathers and mothers of the Church. Having thoroughly ingested that tradition, he was, perhaps, in a unique position to say he would thereafter proceed "by Scripture alone." We and our interpretations, on the other hand, might fare better with a little company.

Dichotomies—I'm thinking—are probably not always false, but they are certainly always fictive. A dichotomy becomes false and misleading only when we imagine it to be more than the tool that it is: a way to *talk about* two parts of a whole. We generally suffer from taking too seriously the distinctions between, say, *faith* and *works*, *body* and *spirit*, perhaps even *life* and *death*, this world and the next.

In our current spiritual pinch—smarting between tradition and Scripture—it is good to remember (and to point out to our fellow travelers) that our Scriptures were composed by and, later, determined by many of those same saintly characters we refer to collectively as the tradition. Not to put too fine a point on it: the tradition preceded—and thereafter equipped us with—the Scriptures.

Jewish readers and the more liturgically canny among Christian readers won't apprehend much of a conflict here, nor much of a surprise. They generally know that the Hebrew Bible is itself comprised of both Scripture *and* tradition, each speaking to the other in an endlessly provocative, continuously generative conversation. Most notably, the Torah—our *Scripture proper*—is understood to have been, even in its initial transmission by God to Moses, attended by an oral accompaniment, which has continued as an attendant tradition.

In an age when so many competing ecclesiastical enterprises—the small, the large, the enormous—are busily chipping out endless lines of new and improved wheels—none of which seem to roll quite so roundly as the original—we would do well to gear up with our thus-far-squandered inheritance before we take to the road.

This book offers some of that tradition, and its purpose is to make available—in what I hope is a pleasing form—some of the spiritual guidance offered by the mothers and fathers who have walked this particular *Way* before us. Their words have been rendered here in verse, and—one prays—in poetry as well. It is safe to say that the originals were all poetry, though they were not all verse. I have re-translated where I both could and felt that I should; I have "adapted" virtually everywhere else, hoping to press a range of existing—and what I took to be insufficiently suggestive—translations into more generous terms, whose evocative figurations might yet come into play, yielding more rather than less.

There is one word, even so, that I have decided for the most part not to translate at all, hoping that we all might acquire a renewed sense of the word itself, and hoping we might dodge the diminishments of its uniformly unsatisfactory translations. This word is *nous*. *Noetic* prayer is the heart of our matter; if it is acquired and sustained, it becomes the means by which we apprehend God's presence and His will. *Nous* is a tasty noun from which the adjective *noetic* springs—a word found throughout the Greek New Testament and throughout the writings of the fathers and mothers of the Church. In translation, its import as, say, *the intellective aptitude of the heart** is almost invariably lost. It is the center of the human person, where mind and matter meet

*Bishop Kallistos Ware, *The Orthodox Way* (Crestwood, NY: St. Vladimir's Seminary Press, 1995).

most profoundly, and where the human person is mystically united to others and to God. I have written elsewhere that "an individual does not a person make." Personhood—if the Image of God is relevant here—is revealed in relationship, and the *nous* is the faculty that enables and performs just such relationship. It can be soiled, both obscured and obscuring, or—if reconstituted and cleansed by God's grace—it can be the faculty by which His presence and will are most clearly known.

Even so, the word is most often rendered as *mind* or *reason* or *intellect*, and these curious choices have become complicit in one of our unfortunate dichotomies, that of the human person into a two-part invention: a relatively deplorable vehicle (the body) and its somewhat more laudable and worthy passenger (the soul or spirit). Along with an insidious (and dusty) doctrine of secret, saving knowledge given to those whose spirits have transcended bodily bondage, this very dichotomy is, frankly, such a dire misunderstanding as to constitute its own species of the Gnostic heresy. You might recognize its legacy as an ongoing, body-bashing error among a good bit of the Western Church, both high and low. A rediscovery of *nous*, therefore, would be a very good thing.

I had been thinking, similarly, to render *psyche* untranslated, but finally decided that *soul*—its familiar stand-in—would have to serve, given that *psyche* has, in the modern era, acquired a good bit of not-so-efficacious accoutrements.

Prologue

Late Request

With love's confidence I'm asking,
    if you should offer this book
        to another, ask of him
as now I ask of you
    to read slowly,
        and thoroughly, tasting
each word's trouble.

    Without doubt, certain passages
        should never stand alone,
but will require assistance
    offered by others to further
        endow their meaning. I fear
for the reader who dabbles,
    who gleans, who hurries to take
        and flee, and who by doing so acquires
nothing but a novel form
    of his current poverty and error.

—*Anonymous author of* The Cloud of Unknowing

ENDLESS LIFE
poems of the mystics

Saint Paul the Apostle
(c. 5–69)

Persecutor-turned-martyr and apostle to the gentiles, Saint Paul was also a true visionary, having mystically experienced the resurrected Christ on the road to Damascus, and having experienced a vision of, as he would say, "the third heaven." His mysticism is both subtle and pervasive, if offered matter-of-factly throughout his several epistles to communities of the early church.

∽ Beyond Knowing

I'll bet your wits won't let you
quite believe any of this; it is, however,
precisely so.

I know a man, a follower of Christ,
who, some fourteen years ago,
was lifted clean

to the third heaven—whether this
occurred in the body or out of it,
I could not say,

though God knows. And this same man—
whether in the body or out of it,
I do not know,

though God surely knows—was lifted
(hear me!) clean to Paradise, and there
he heard such words

—so marvelous and grave—that no
human tongue could repeat them,
nor think to try.

∽ *Love's Body*

Lean in! I was a child, and spoke like one;
　　　My thought? very like a child's.
　　　　　I gripped my reason with both
my little fists. It smelled suspiciously of milk.
　　　Now, as a man, I've learned to let it go.
　　　　　Just now, we squint to see the Image through
this latent, bleak obscurity. One day, we'll see the Image—
　　　as Himself—gleaming from each face.
　　　　　Just now, I puzzle through a range
of incoherencies; but on that day,
　　　the scattered fragments will cohere.
　　　　　In all of this, both now and ever,
faith and hope and love abide, these
　　　sacred three, but the greatest of these (you surely
　　　　　must have guessed) is love.

Saint Irenaeus
(c. 125–c. 210)

The polemic writings of Irenaeus may have laid the foundations of much Christian theology, especially Orthodox Christology. Born in one of the maritime provinces of Asia Minor and liberally educated in both the Scriptures and Greek philosophy and poetry, he offered a vision that defended the early Church from a good deal of philosophical speculation, in particular those errors imported by Gnosticism. He was particularly moved by the teachings and the example of Saint Polycarp.

∽ Capable Flesh

The tender flesh itself
    will be found one day
—quite surprisingly—
    to be capable of receiving,
and yes, full
    capable of embracing
the searing energies of God.
    Go figure. Fear not.
For even at its beginning
    the humble clay received
God's art, whereby
    one part became the eye,
another the ear, and yet
    another this impetuous hand.
Therefore, the flesh
    is not to be excluded

from the wisdom and the power
    that now and ever animates
all things. His life-giving
    agency is made perfect,
we are told, in weakness—
    made perfect in the flesh.

∽ *The Human Person*

1.
Well *no*! the body is not itself
    the soul—though, *yes*, apparently
it may partake of soul in this our
    complicated interim—and you
probably shouldn't take the soul
    for *life*, say, but here again,
the soul presumably enjoys
    a share of the essential, animating
life God gives. For instance, Adam
    "was made a living soul."
It is by sharing in the *Life that Is*
    that every soul is quickened. Still,
I see that life and soul are these days
    separate things. Thus it is
when God gives life, the souls
    which held no previous existence
begin from that moment and obtain
    a permanence, a thereafter perpetual

duration. It is God who wills them, first,
    to be and, thereafter, to continue to become.

2.
Soul and spirit may be your parts,
but they are not your all. As for the *you*
entire? A mixture and a gathering: a soul

receiving the Spirit of the Father, joined
to flesh graved in His image. Lose the clay
and what you have is not a *spiritual man*

but something more like *bodiless spirit of a man.*
Still, when Spirit, sweetly blended with a soul, unites
with God-shaped clay, you find then striding

in unique beauty a spiritual and complete
man or woman, made to bear, in lush company,
both the image and the likeness of the God.

Saint Melito of Sardis
(† c. 190)

Saint Melito, who lived and served near Smyrna in Asia Minor, is understood to have been an Apostolic Father who, in all likelihood, knew both Saints Polycarp and Irenaeus. He is sometimes called Bishop of Sardis, Bishop of Ittica, and "the Philosopher." His best-known work is a mystical treatise on Holy Pascha, the central feast of the Church, better known in the West as Easter.

◦ Pascha, our Passing over into Life

Finally! The Hebrew Scriptures have been opened
and the mystery declared:
how the sheep was sacrificed, and how
a people were redeemed,
and Pharaoh wincing, lashed by unsuspected mystery.

Therefore, all-belovéd, apprehend
the secrets of the Pascha.
See that they contain both new and old,
eternal and provisional,
what passes and what will never pass away,
mortal and immortal, both.

For the law is old, but the world—have you noticed?—
is suddenly new; the figure is
provisional, while grace is everlasting.
The trembling sheep is mortal,
but the Lord—unbroken as the lamb, raised up
by God's sure hand, is deathless.

⤜ Christ Speaks

It is I, speaks the Christ, *I am he*
who puts Death to death, and stands above
the fallen enemy, crushes Hades
to bland chalk, binds the dark powers, and bears
all humankind up to heavenly peaks.
Yes, says Christ, *I am he.*

Therefore come, all human families
ruined by sin, and receive absolution
of every error. I am your liberation
and the passage of deliverance.
I am the throat-cut lamb and sacrifice,
your ransom paid, your pulse and life, your fire,
your rescue, resurrection, and your king.
I gather you in one strong hand,
and guide you to the heights of paradise,
where I will show to you your Father.

⤜ How It Was

The earth trembled; its foundations
shook like silt; the sun, chagrined,
fled the scene, and every mundane
element scattered in retreat. The day
became the night: for light could not endure
the image of the Master hanging on a tree.

All creation was astonished, perplexed
and stammering, *What new mystery is this?*
The Judge is judged, and yet He holds his peace;
the Invisible One is utterly exposed, and yet
is not ashamed; the Incomprehensible is grasped,
and will not turn indignant; the Immensity
is circumscribed, and acquiesces; the absolutely
Unattainable suffers, and yet does not avenge;
the Immortal dies, and utters not a word;
the Celestial is pressed into the earthen grave,
and He endures! What new mystery is this?
The whole creation, I say, was astonished;
but, when our Lord stood up in Hades—
trampling death underfoot, subduing
the strong one, setting every captive free—
then all creation saw clearly that for its sake
the Judge was condemned, et cetera.
For our Lord, even when He deigned
to be born, was condemned in order
that He might show mercy, was bound
that He might loose, was seized
that He might release, suffered
that He might show compassion, died
that He might give life, was laid in the grave
that He might rise, might raise.

Origen of Alexandria
(182–251)

Origen of Alexandria is beloved as one of the greatest of Christian theologians. As a philosopher, he is perhaps best known for his Neoplatonist treatise On First Principles. *An incisive critic of pagan philosophy, he nonetheless adapted its most useful and attractive teachings to further expound the Orthodox Christian faith.*

∞ Of Us All

One God and Father of us all, who is above all and through all and in all.
—*Ephesians 4:6*

As with any giddy-making Mystery
you might hope to grip, in part
to apprehend, you'll have to settle
for a relatively local image to suggest
the God's surpassing all-sufficiency.
The sun, say, by its obvious position,
is patently *above all* things that crowd
our blue-green globe, and by its rays
it can be said to shine *through all.*
And more: when the power of its light
has pierced through every depth,
it is said thereby to be *in all.* In just
this way, we might surmise—in keeping
with our spinning apprehensions—
that its supremacy is underscored

by the words *above all*, and its sufficiency
for every being in the *through all*,
and still the coming of the power
of God made manifest in the *in all*.
The result, then, is
that no one is found, ever,
to be empty, due to our God's
truly being, and of His being *all in all*.

∽ *All in All*

In this way, (and note) accordingly,
we might suppose that at the someday
consummation—what I would call
the promised restoration of all things—
those who make their gradual advance,
as well as those ascending
will step surprised into that land, into
the healing action of its elements.
Here, each will be prepared for all
immense occasions to which
nothing further can be added.
And here, the King of all, Himself,
will school each blinking creature
in this the holy enterprise, instructing
all and reigning *in* them 'til He has
led them wholly to the Father—who
you'll find has joined all things to Himself

—that is, until they are made capable
of receiving God, so that the God
may ever be to them The All in All.

Saint Athanasios
(c. 298–373)

*Patriarch of his native Alexandria, Saint Athanasios spent 17 years in
exile because his unflinching faith in the divinity of Christ compelled him
to refuse and to continue to refute the then-popular Arian heresy, which
claimed Christ to be merely a created being. Besides his famous work* On
the Incarnation, *his* Life of Saint Antony *is also widely admired.*

৯৶ The Invisible Seen

When our dull wits had so declined
as to set us mid the squalor of the merely
sensible creation, the Very God consented
to become a body of His own, that He
as one among us might gather our dim senses
to Himself, and manifest through such
incommensurate occasion that He
is not simply man, but also God,
the Word and Wisdom of the One.

Thereafter, He remained His body, and thus
allowed Himself to be observed.
His becoming joined to us performed
two appalling works in our behalf:

He banished death from these
our tendered frames, and made of them
something new and (take note here) renewing.

∽ *The Death of Death*

Put fear aside. Now
    that He has entered
into death on our behalf,
    all who live
no longer die
    as men once died.

That ephemeral occasion
    has met its utter end.
As seeds cast to the earth, we
    will not perish,
but like those seeds
    shall rise again—the shroud
of death itself having been
    burst to tatters
by love's immensity.

∽ *His Image Recovered*

So—and yes, I'm asking—what was the God to do?
What other course—His being God and All—but to renew
His lately none-too-vivid Image in the aspect of mankind,
so that, by His Icon thus restored, we dim occasions might
once more come to know Him? And how should this be done,
save by the awful advent of the very God Himself, our Lord
and King and gleaming Liberator Jesus Christ?

Here, belovéd numbskulls, is a little picture: You gather,
one presumes, what must be done when a portrait on a panel
becomes obscured—maybe even lost—to external stain.
The artist does not discard the panel, though the subject must return
to sit for it again, whereupon the likeness is etched once more upon
the same material. As He tells us in the Gospel, *I came*
to seek and to save that which was lost—our faces, say.

As a Good Teacher

He schools us as a canny teacher condescends
to hunker face to face with his more or less
ungainly pupils, settling down to their level,
employing whatever means prove meet. As we
had turned from *cosmos*—the beauty above, light-laden—
and sought Him in the muck among created things,
the God in His great love took to Himself an earthen body;
or rather, He *became* one—and moved as Man among men,
meeting our slow senses, as it were, midway.

Scant Offering

Here, then, our meager alms
to you who love the Christ.
These words may give you
a beginning, though you must
go on to live their truth
by performing the Scriptures.
Any likely apprehension
of those texts requires first
an honest life, a limpid soul, and yes,
a Christ-like virtue well-obtained . . .
and all this long before the eye
can glimpse—so far as human nature
will allow—the truth concerning
God the Word. I wonder, would

you rush to look upon so much
as a sunlit morning without first
rubbing sleep-set grit from your eye?
And should you wish to see
a distant country, won't you first
prepare the journey and then,
thus girded, make your slogging
way to it? Just so, anyone desiring
to know the minds of those
whose hands have given us
the Scriptures must first address
his own life, and so approach
the saints by imitation of their acts.

Saint Ephraim of Syria
(† 373)

Best known for his psalmody and for the penitential prayer bearing his name, Saint Ephraim served as teacher of Christians and counselor to bishops in and around Nisibis, until the year 363, when he and his community were forced to relocate to Edessa, where the saint continued to serve the people and his bishop until his death ten years later.

∾ The Prayer of Saint Ephraim

O Lord and Master of my life,
remove from me this languid spirit,
this grim demeanor, this petty

lust for power, and all this empty talk.
Endow Thy servant, instead,
with a chaste spirit, a humble
heart, longsuffering gentleness,
and genuine, unselfish love.

Yes, O Lord and King, grant
that I may confront my own offenses,
and remember not to judge my brother.
For You are—always and forever—blessed.

◌◡ *Due Praise*

Glory to You, Only Lover of mankind!
Glory to You, O Merciful!
Glory to You, O Longsuffering!
Glory to You, who forgive every error!
Glory to You, who descended to save our souls!
Glory to You, made flesh in the Virgin's womb!
Glory to You, who were bound!
Glory to You, who were torn!
Glory to you, who were crucified!
Glory to you, who were buried!
Glory to you, who did rise!
Glory to you, who were proclaimed!
Glory to you, who were believed!
Glory to you, who were taken up!
Glory to you, who are gloriously enthroned

at the Father's right hand, soon to return
with the glory of the Father and the holy Angels
to measure every soul that has reviled
Your holy sufferings.
In that fearful hour,
when the powers of heaven will be shaken;
when Angels, Archangels, Cherubim, and Seraphim
will arrive together with fear and trembling
before Your glory; when the foundations
of creation will shudder, and everything
that has breath will tremble at Your great,
unendurable glory.
In that hour, Your hand will cover me
as a great protecting wing, and my soul
will be rescued from the fire, the gnashing
teeth, the swirling chaos without light,
the endless weeping,
so that, blessing You, I may say,
Glory to the One who sank to save the sinking sinner.

Two trees the God was pleased
      to place in Paradise—the lace-leafed
      Tree of Life and the generously
      overreaching Tree of Wisdom—as a pair
      of blesséd fountains and the source
      of every good. By means of these
      the pilgrim is persuaded to become
      the very likeness of God, endowed
      with life that does not end,
      with wisdom that does not err.

If you, even in your condition, would partake
      of the future Kingdom, first pursue
      the Sovereign's favor *here*. In keeping
      with the measure by which you choose
      to honor Him, He is sure to honor you.
      How you serve just now is how that land
      will serve you then. Give Him all
      your soul that He will see you now
      and ever worthy of a saint's esteem.

If you were to ask *How may I acquire*
      His benevolence? try this: Bring Him
      gold and silver through the needy.
      If you're short on cash, bring Him
      faith and love and temperance,
      bring Him calm, and kindness, most

of all a humble heart. Take great care
not to judge—not anyone, protect
your eyes from vanity, keep your hand
from doing wrong, and keep
your foot from unlikely paths.
And while you're at it: Comfort the countless
frightened, console all who suffer.
At the very least, get off their backs.
Lift the cup to those who thirst, and break
a little bread to feed the hungry.
You know this all already; now do it.

∾ The Living Bread

His holy body wholly mixed
   with these our bodies, and His pure
      blood poured generously out
to fill our veins, His voice
   now pulses in our ears,
      and look! His lighted vision
pools within our eyes. All of Him
   is mixed with all of us—
      compassionate communion. And as
He loves His church His body
   utterly, so He gives
      it more than bread, more
even than bread from heaven,
   but gives His own, His
      living Bread for her to eat.

Wheat, the olive, and the grape—
    these three—serve Your mystic union
            in threefold manner.
Your bread became our strength,
    Your wine our consolation.
            Our faces were renewed,
illumined by the grace and
    blessing of Your holy oil. For all
            of this and more, Your body—
saved by Your abasement—
    now unites in true thanksgiving.
            And Death—the insatiable lion
who consumed us all—by You alone
    its appetite was sated, by You alone
            its hold has burst, and we
rise strengthened, comforted, luminous.

∽ *The Messenger Who Came*

Blesséd is the Messenger who came,
bearing as He strove a lasting peace.
By mercy of the Father, He's appeared,
lowering His brow to meet us here, and here
has squared His Lordship with His people.

            Glory to your rising in the East,
            both human and divine.

Blesséd is the Wisdom who allied
the dying with the One Who Lives, and so
has joined the highest to the low, and so
commingled tinctures to a shade
now fit, restoring His own Image to the clay.

> Glory to your rising in the East,
> divine and human.

Blesséd is He, Compassionate, who saw
the pathway blocked, the flaming spear
obstructing still our journey to the Tree of Life—
that by opening His unprotected side,
which, pierced, sufficed to open Paradise.

> Glory to your rising in the East,
> both human and divine.

∾ What Bides Waiting

The fragrant air of Paradise returns
        the agéd to their youth. Its scented
                breeze awakens in their wearied bodies
the rising pulse of spring. In that land,
        all stain submerges to a sudden blush.

In the fallen face of Moses on that final mount,
        you might see the God has traced a parabolic icon
                of just what lies ahead: his ashen cheeks, scored
by age and error, became luminous and fair.

All who wake to find themselves
    in Paradise awaken pure, for they
        have left all pettiness behind;
no anger mars their faces,
    ferocity fallen clean away;
        they bear no mocking disposition,
for scorn has fallen short.
    Because they do no harm,
        they do not harm themselves.
All past hatreds, envies, and regrets
    fail to figure in their thought.
        As new, renewing creatures, each
beholds himself in glory,
    and in wonder walks beholding
        other beauties similarly walking.
The very nature of the body
    —once troubled and troubling—
        has quieted, resplendent
outwardly in beauty, inwardly
    in innocence—the body in ways evident,
        the soul in hidden measure, ever so.

Saint Syncletica of Alexandria
(c. 316–c. 400)

Among the desert abbas and ammas (fathers and mothers) of the church in Egypt, one of the most revered was Amma Syncletica. Upon the death of her parents, the saint cut her hair and moved with her blind sister to commence a life of ascesis in the family tomb. Somewhat under duress, she became the spiritual mentor of many female disciples who had moved to the desert to pursue lives of prayer.

✍ Sayings

As you begin this eternal movement toward God
you'll find struggle and no shortage of suffering.
And afterwards, ineffable joy.

Those who would ignite a fire are at first
choked by smoke, their eyes stinging
with hot tears. Even so, by this effort
they obtain what they have sought:
The God Who is a consuming fire.

Just so, we kindle this divine fire
with tears and breath and labor.

* * *

The most bitter medicines
purge the body of its illness.
Prayer coupled with fasting
drives evil thoughts away.

* * *

We sail through a cloud of darkness.

* * *

There is a grief that assists,
and a grief that destroys.
The first is revealed
by tears for our failings
and for our neighbors' frailty.
The second manifests
in despair and apathy;
this one must be cast aside,
by prayer and psalmody.

* * *

The flitting bird abandons the nest,
and so her eggs never hatch.
The monk or nun grows cold
and faith dies, when the monastic
wanders from place to place.

* * *

For those who are capable of poverty,
it is a perfect good.

* * *

Rejoice that God visits you. Keep
this blessing on your lips:
You were iron, but fire

has purged the rust from you.
The righteous who fall ill,
will rise from strength to strength.
You are gold! You will pass through fire, pure.
Have you a thorn in the flesh? Be glad!
You are honored, even as Saint Paul.
Are you being schooled by fever?
Are you being tested by cold?
You have drawn the first lot;
be ready for the second.
With a loud voice, offer holy words.
The Holy One hears when you call!
Open your mouth all the wider
to be taught by these exercises of the soul.

Saint Makarios of Egypt
(c. 283–390)

Widowed as a young man, the saint sought a life comprised entirely of prayer. Of his 90-something years, fully 60 were spent in the desert wilderness conversing with God. He left behind some fifty ascetical homilies and several "ascetic tracts," for the purpose of assisting others who would attain to a life of prayer. Several of his prayers are included in certain matins and vespers services of the Eastern Church.

∽ Awaiting Prayer

Well yes, we have a need to pray, though not
so much a prayer that's fixed to any habit
of the body, nor to any public proclamation,
nor tied to some particular custom
of silence, and not necessarily fallen
to our aching knees. Rather, we ought
first to keep an attentive mind, leaning in
expectantly, and waiting on the God
until He comes visiting the soul, making
mysterious entry via any manner of
countless paths—the openings
and varied senses of the soul. Just so,
we should be silent when we ought,
or, on occasion, raise a piercing cry,
or bruise our knees on stone—whatever—
so long as the mind is attached wholly
to God's approach. As the body, performing
any demanding task, requires every member

to join in fixed attention to the chore, so
the soul demands such singleness
of rapt pursuit, in loving movement
to the Lord—undistracted, undeterred, but firm
and watchful, expecting His arrival, even now.

∽ The Human Soul

Do not, best belovéd, consider lightly
    the intellective value of the soul.
The human soul, immortal—of itself
    a precious vessel—has obtained
the God's inestimable love. Witness
    the glory of the heavens and the earth,
and know that God took little pleasure
    in them, preferring you. And note
your worth to Him, considering
    how—not for the sake of angels,
but for you—He came to your assistance,
    called you back when you were lost,
when you were wounded, ill, and how
    He then restored you to your first, created
state—as righteous Eve and Adam savoring
    the garden, unencumbered, unimpaired, free
of mark or stain.

ꞈ A Union

Best belovéd, all good things are held
intricately bound to one another.
Prayer is bound to love, and love to joy.
Joy avails meekness, and meekness feeds
humility. Humility leads to service, just
as service offers hope. Hope shores up
our faith, and faith obtains obedience,
which becomes a newfound liberty.

The vices are also thus, precisely
intertwined. *Any* hatred disposes one
to anger, anger leads to pride, and pride
feeds all manner of vainglory, which,
in turn, occasions disbelief. Disbelief
will turn your heart to stone, and that
stone heart allows a blithe, recurrent
carelessness attaining to a state
of sloth. Sloth is the root of apathy,
which makes endurance moot.
And while this lack of perseverance may
lead to love, it is a heartless love of pleasure.

In all of this, the head of every good
endeavor bides in persevering prayer.
By means of this great gift—immediate
audience with the King of all—we avoid
the chain of vice and we gain all virtues,
simply leaning in to ask that they be given us.

Saint Macrina the Younger
(c. 327–379)

The eldest of ten children, the daughter, granddaughter and sister of saints, Saint Macrina is credited by her brothers—Saints Basil the Great and Gregory of Nyssa—as having been the one whose example and counsel led them to put aside earthly pursuits in favor of service to God. With her brother, Saint Peter of Sebaste, the saint founded twin communities—a women's convent and a men's monastery—on opposite banks of the River Iris. It was in this convent that Saint Macrina pursued a life of prayer, accompanied by her mother and many other ascetic women.

∽ Prayers

1.
You free us from the dread of death,
and make this life a door. You grant
our very flesh a fallow season,
then gather all at the last horn's blast.
You sow the earth with these our bodies,
shaped by Your own Hand. You bring
the harvest in, transforming death into
abundant life, all defect into beauty.

Bearing our curse, becoming sin,
You loose us from both the burden
of the law and from our lawlessness.
You bruise the serpent's head,
and snatch us from its grip. You open
the way to resurrection, shattering

the gates of hell. You slay the one
who held death's power, give comfort
to those who honor You. You give the holy cross
by which our enemy is slain, by which
our life returns to us abundantly.

2.

Most Holy God, into Whose Hands
I was born, Beloved of my soul, to whom
I have offered my consecrated flesh
since even my earliest days, entrust me
to a luminous angel, who will lift
my hand to guide me to the place
where I may drink, and rest, and gain
my strength in the embrace of my holy fathers.

3.

You Who shattered the fire of the flaming sword,
Who gathered to paradise—for the sake of his plea
for pity—the thief crucified by Your side,
remember me also in Your kingdom.
I too have been crucified with You.
For fear of You, I have nailed down my flesh,
trembling as I await your judgments.

4.

Please, may the horrible abyss not separate
me from those you have redeemed.
Please, may the corrupt, corrupting enemy

not hinder my path to You.
Please, if by any human weakness
I have sinned in word or deed or thought,
may my sin pass unnoticed by Your sight.

5.
Please, O Holy One with power to forgive,
forgive me. May I awaken that day drawing breath,
and revive within Your Holy Presence, having shed
every ill of the flesh, and *without spot or wrinkle*
as a replenished soul be received by Your hand,
rising to You as incense.

Saint Basil the Great
(329–379)

The Archbishop of Caesarea, Saint Basil is revered—together with Saints John Chrysostom and Gregory Nazianzos—as one of the "Three Holy Hierarchs" of the Church. Together with that same Nazianzos and Saint Gregory of Nyssa, Saint Basil is revered as one the "Cappadocian Fathers," whose homiletical and mystical writings helped establish what is now considered the heart of Orthodox theology and spirituality. As Saint Benedict is honored for founding monasticism in the West, Saint Basil is honored for founding monasticism in the East. The Divine Liturgy bearing his name is the central Eucharistic service of the Eastern Church throughout Great Lent, Christmas, Theophany, and on the saint's feast day, January 1.

∽ Illumination

If we are illumined
    by His divine agency, and fix
        our eyes upon the beauty
of the image making manifest
    our invisible God,
        and if, by that image,
we are allowed to glimpse
    the inexpressible
        beauty of its source,
it is because
    we have already become
        utterly joined to the Spirit.

The Holy One pours out
upon those who love
the vision of the truth
a power that enables
them to see the image—
and this power is Himself.

∽ A Prayer

Master over every Power,
Shaper of all that is, Holy One
who, in dreadful compassion
and dire mercy, chose
to send Your Only Son,
Jesus Christ our Lord,
for the recovery of mankind,
and with His very Cross ripped
to tatters the record of our sins,
silencing the powers of the dark:
O Most Merciful, receive
from your errant creatures
these words of gratitude and these
of supplication, and deliver us
from every hurtful error,
and from all seen and unseen enemies
who seek our harm. Nail down
our flesh with fear of You,

and keep our hearts tipped well away
from words or thoughts of evil.
Pierce our souls with love,
so that—attending to You always, being
lighted by You, and glimpsing You,
O unapproachable, everlasting
Light—we may ever offer
confession and speak
our joyful thanks to You:
The eternal Father,
with Your Only-Begotten Son,
and with Your All-Holy,
Gracious, Life-Giving Spirit,
now and ever, and unto
everlasting ages. Amen.

Saint Gregory Nazianzos
(330–389)

Also known as Saint Gregory the Theologian, the saint is revered as one of the "Three Holy Hierarchs" of the Church as well as one of the "Cappadocian Fathers," whose homiletical and mystical writings helped establish what is now considered the heart of Orthodox theology and spirituality. He shares the designation of Theologian with only two other mystics, Saint John the Divine and Saint Symeon the New.

✑ The Shepherd

Think again, and even now, how
    the famous Shepherd—the One
who lays His life down for His sheep,
    came pressing sore to find
the solo agent straying, lost
    upon the mountain's rugged hills,
how He found that wanderer, and having
    found it, bore it firmly
on His shoulders and, having done so,
    schlepped it back
to its blinking, live community.
    Having set it right, He numbered it
among the sheep who never strayed.
    A figure then, a puzzle: He lit
a candle—see, His very Flesh—and swept
    an unkempt house, cleansing

all the world of contagion. He sought
    the precious coin whose Royal
Image was obscured by stain.
        Listen. Ever—now—He calls together
all His friends the angels
    upon the finding of that coin,
and makes them all partakers in His joy.

The Soul's Permanence

I'm asking. If the soul—the breath
of God—has suffered by its being
both a heavenly and an earthly
element (as, say, a light might be
concealed in a cave), it remains
in any case divine, immortal.

Spiritual Being

And even now—as, say, within
a forest clearing, rain-laced air combines
with sun's bright energies to spin
the many-colored rainbow, and so extend
illuminating elements in an arc
to span great distances—just so
the energies exuding from the One
Great Light insist on reaching
with its rays every lesser intellect.

He is—we are quite right to say—
the fountain of all lights, and sends
them flowing without fail, especially
the Light we cannot name, nor grasp,
the Light eluding all reductive terms,
forever racing far beyond our wits,
so that, with strong desire, we
might struggle all the more to touch
what extends so far beyond us.

Saint Gregory of Nyssa
(c. 335–395)

Saint Gregory, Bishop of Nyssa, was the third of the three "Cappadocian Fathers," whose homilectical and mystical writings helped to shape Orthodox theology and spirituality. Somewhat overshadowed by his brother, Saint Basil the Great, and by that brother's great friend, Saint Gregory Nazianzos, the saint is nonetheless revered for his mystical writings, especially those exploring typologically the life of Moses. His "life" of his sister, Saint Macrina, is exemplary of early church hagiography.

☙ *His Death Our Life*

Here's the sacred issue: He came so close
to our decay, so close as to mix our nature
newly with His own, and thus provide
to our poor clay His endless resurrection.

∾ Soul's Eternal Rapture

The soul that looks
      finally to God, conceives
            a new, mouth-watering
desire for His
      eternal beauty,
            and tasting this, she
awakens to an ever
      greater yearning—
            an ache never
to be fully satisfied.

By this sweet hurt,
      she never ceases
            to extend herself,
to touch those things
      beyond her reach
            and ever beckoning.
By this she finds herself
      passing, always,
            from her present
circumstance to enter
      more deeply the interior,
            and to find
there yet another
      circumstance awaiting.

And thus, at every point
      she learns that each
            new splendor is to be
eclipsed by what will come—
      the ever-exceeding
            Beautiful that draws, and calls,
and leads the belovéd
      to a beauty of her own.

∽ Allegory of the Soul

The soul has followed Moses and the cloud,
for both will serve as guides for those who cross
the burning desert eager to advance
in what we hope to apprehend as virtue.

As Moses walks—the letter of the law,
leading him the cloud proceeds as law's
spiritual accompaniment. The shining soul,
new-cleansed by its late crossing of the Sea,
has purged all sinful remnants from itself
and has destroyed the army in pursuit.
It took the bitter waters which turned sweet
by having met the mystery of wood.

Among the unmatched beauty of oasis palms, soul
fills itself with waters, mystically supplied.
It takes the bread of heaven to its lips, and so

becomes itself, defeats the foreign host
beneath the lawgiver's high and cruciform embrace.

From there, the soul proceeds, enters country
promised long ago, enabled now and finally
to attend and to enjoy the mystery of Sacred Being.

Mother Theodora of Egypt
(c. 340–c. 410)

A true "amma" of the desert, Mother Theodora served as colleague and confidant to Archbishop Theophilos of Alexandria. Her life seems to have been focused upon developing a life of prayer and upon assisting her many disciples in developing similarly dynamic prayer lives. Acutely aware of the struggle to fend off melancholy and despair, she is one of the first of the mothers and fathers to describe that devastating state of spiritual torpor called acedia, *and among the first to offer effective defenses against it.*

∽ Sayings

Come, together we will press
to enter the camel's eye,
that narrowest of gates.

Observe the trees. Just as they
must endure the winter's storms
before they can bear fruit, so it is

with us. This troubled age is our own
destructive storm. Enduring
its trials and temptations, we obtain
our inheritance, our flowering, this new
fruitfulness, and also enter heaven's kingdom.

And, true enough, it is good
to live in peace, praying ceaselessly.
It is very good for the ascetics
to live in peace, especially
the young ones. Take care,
even so, for as soon as you set out
to live in peace, that is when
the enemy takes notice, and will
attack with forces great and small.
Be quick to seek assistance, and
guard your heart, especially
against the small.

I know a monk, who, because of many
temptations said, *I will go away from here.*
As he laced his sandals, he saw another monk
also lacing up his sandals, and this other said to him,
Is it on my account that you are going?
Because I go before you wherever you walk.

Neither asceticism, nor vigils
nor any manner of suffering can save,
only genuine humility will serve.

I know an anchorite able to banish demons;
he asked them, *What makes you go away?*
Is it fasting? They replied, *We do not eat or drink.*
Is it vigils? They said, *We do not sleep.*
Is it separation from the world?
They answered, *We thrive in deserts.*
What power sends you away?
They said, *Nothing overcomes us, save humility.*

Saint Augustine of Hippo
(354–430)

*Saint Augustine was one of the chief figures in the theology of the Church
in the West. Many Protestants, especially those in the lineage of Calvin,
consider him to be one of the primary sources of theological teaching
on salvation and grace. He was born in Africa—the eldest son of Saint
Monica—was educated in Rome, and was baptized as an adult in Milan.
His best known work,* The Confessions, *is considered the first Western
autobiography.*

∽ A Speculation

Plato says that souls cannot exist
without their bodies. And Porphyry
contends that souls purified—having renewed
communion with the Father—shall never
return to the world's anguishing infirmities.

If Plato speaks what truth he saw—that souls,
though pure and perfect, and belonging
to the righteous and the wise, must return
to human bodies—and if Porphyry, again,
has imparted the bit of truth he came to know—
that blesséd souls shall never see again
the miseries obtained within corrupting
bodies—then we, as they, should see
the brother truth—that souls indeed return
to the sweet animality of body, and also
that these bodies be endowed then
with the mystery of immortal life.

∽ The Beatific Vision

Consider, as you may—or as the God
may now allow you—how the holy ones
will be employed when they are then
arrayed in deathless bodies, when the very
flesh shall shine, having vanquished all decay.
To tell the truth, I'm at a loss to understand
how this will be, but I have faith in those
who bear witness. Doubtless, this surpasses
all understanding save His own. Still, we
shall one day, and miraculously, participate
in His radiant peace, within ourselves, and with
our neighbors, and—dare to trust it!—
with the God. Remember how great a man

he was who gave his witness thus: *We know*
in part, and we prophesy in part, until
that which is perfect arrives, and more,
Now we see as through a glass, darkly,
but then and suddenly face to face.
So now, when I am asked how the holy
shall be employed in that incorruptible
body, I do not say what I see, but say
what I believe, according to what I find
written in the psalm, *I believed, and therefore*
have I spoken. I say, then, that they shall see
the God unfailingly before them.

⚬ Soul's Purpose

> *Thou hast formed us*
> *for Thyself, and so our hearts*
> *are ever restless till they find*
> *their rest in Thee.*

How, O God, will I find my rest in You? When
will You come flowing to my heart that it may be
absolutely drenched, that, drunk with you, I may
forget my sorrows, knowing only your embrace,
my one and only good, O lover of mankind?

Help me now to glimpse both who and what
You are to me. Extend Your mercy. Give me words
that I may speak, and hear the words I say. What am I

that You demand my love? What am I that my withholding
brings such pain? Teach me the compassion of Your name.

Say unto my soul, *I am thy salvation.* Speak that I may hear.
Behold, my heart lies open before You, awaiting
Your word. Open me sufficiently to hear You say
to my soul, *I am thy salvation.* And when, hearing You,
I run to grasp You, do not hide Your face from me.

Or let me die, if I must die, if only I might see Your face.

∞ *Prayer*

Here and now—why not?—let
there rise—even as You
provide it, even as You grant
both pleasure and ability—let
there spring, at long last, truth
from the earth, and let joy
in finally *doing* something
settle on us from heaven.

Yes, we have thought good
thoughts, and guessed
good thoughts were plenty.
High time for a little light
in the firmament. High time
we did as we thought, did
as we said. Help us.

And look! New fruit
leaps from the earth,
and this because the earth
is good. May we see
our momentary light
burst forth and—born
of good work and the sweet
savor of contemplation, born
of the Word of Life above—
let us appear as sudden lights,
drawing radiance from the lush
firmament of Your Scripture.

∾ The Eighth Day

It is not for you or me to know the times,
which the Father has kept within His own
benign authority. After the current season
in which we find ourselves, the God shall rest,
as on the seventh day, and there He will give us—
who shall be the seventh day—rest within Himself.

Suffice to say that the seventh shall be
brought to a close, not by an evening,
but yet another day, the Lord's day, as an eighth
and an eternal day, consecrated by the radiating
resurrection of Christ, and prefiguring
the eternal reposition and repose,
not of spirit only, but of the body too.

There we shall rest and see, see and love,
love and praise. This is what shall be
in our exalted end without an end.

Evagrios of Pontos
(345–399)

*Having, through years of desert ascesis, absorbed the spirituality of
Egyptian and Palestinian monasticism, Evagrios labored throughout
his life to transmit that deep beauty to others. His letters, his* Praktikos
(Practical Life), his Chapters on Prayer *and his* Ad Monachos *(To the
Monks) reveal a mystical vision of life in Christ realized, and they reveal
as well a father's devotion to his children, his labor and his prayer for
their well-being.*

∾ Effusions on Prayer

I.
Prayer is the ongoing conversation
of the human spirit with its God.

Yet even Moses could not approach the burning bush
before he had pulled the shoes from his feet.
Free yourself from every passion-clouded thought
if you wish to see the One Who Is beyond them.

* * *

Pray first of all for the gift of tears.
Your sorrow might then soften your natural insolence.

Pray with tears and your heartfelt petitions
will find a hearing. Nothing so moves Him
as a supplication accompanied by tears.

Take care that you do not turn this gift into a curse,
considering yourself superior because you weep.

Focus on the prayer.

The devils will surely suggest distracting matters,
desiring that your mind will search them, and suspecting
failure in prayer you will know chagrin, and lose confidence.

Endeavor to be both deaf and dumb during prayer.
Then you will be able to pray.

II.
Prayer is the manifest blossom of meekness.

Prayer is the fruit of grateful joy.

Prayer fends off despondency.

This is why possessions are a burden,
and why you must take up your cross,
so you can pray at long last without distraction.

* * *

If you would pray, and worthily, lose the shabby
self-concern and your habitual defensiveness.
Endure all things unmoved, for the sake of prayer.

Whatever injustice you endure
silently—and smiling, even—will yield
delicious fruit at the time of prayer.

Any trace of resentment soils
your already cloudy *nous*,
and therefore obscures prayer.

* * *

The one who makes note of injuries and still expects to pray
may as well gather water to store it in a bucket full of holes.

Practice genuine patience, and your prayer
will always taste of joy.

Sure, you can justify your anger—even during prayer—
just know that you have soiled yourself before God.

* * *

Take care that while appearing to correct and heal another
you do not make your own illness incurable.

Spare your righteous indignation and be spared.

Do not simply appear to pray, but bend
your mind, and with great fear.

III.
Do you recall those times when prayer turned sweet
and all disturbing thoughts fled far away?
That was when your angel made his presence known.
At other times, the struggle turns severe, and the spirit
cannot so much as raise its eyes before it's torn
by passions. If, even then, the spirit will continue striving,
prayer will come; knock on the door hard enough
and it will fly open.

IV.
So, you want to pray?
Renounce all things,
and in that way inherit all.

In prayer, ask only that God's will become
your own. Thereafter, all things will be given in a flood.

* * *

It is an essential element of justice
that you should pray not only
for your own cleansing, but for
the cleansing of everyone else.
In this way, you imitate the angels.

Take care, and note if you
truly stand before God
in your prayer, or if you
suffer some compulsion
to be approved by men.
If that is the case, no amount
of prayer becomes
anything other than
a shameful pretext.

* * *

Whether you pray alone or among others, struggle
that your prayer become more than a habit. Make it
a confrontation, and of the moment, now.

If your spirit continues to wander during prayer,
you have not yet learned to pray. You are no better
than a busy man who dabbles in landscape gardening.

> Note: The memory is a powerful distraction during prayer.
> Keep your memory under duress. Do not let it suggest
> again your habitual fancies, but force it to convey
> an awareness of reaching out to God.

V.
Even one who has become quite free
of all the passions may yet fail to truly pray.
> It is not uncommon for a man to have only
> the purest thoughts and yet become so distracted
> by mulling them over that he remains
> far removed from God.

Even when the spirit excels in the avoidance
of these distractions, it does not by that alone
attain the place of prayer.
>It may continue in contemplation of created things,
>and squander time considering their nature.

Even if the spirit manages to rise above
such contemplation of things bodily, it has yet
to see the perfect biding place of God.
>It may still be so absorbed in speculation of what's intelligible
>that it continues to partake of their scattered multiplicity.

Therefore, if you hope to pray, then it is God
you need. He it is who gives prayer to the one who prays.
The one who worships in Spirit and Truth
ceases to honor the Creator because of His works,
but clings to Him because of Himself.

VI.
If you are rightly called a theologian, it is because you truly pray.
If you truly pray, you are rightly called a theologian.

VII.
As your spirit withdraws—one might say—incrementally away
from world-directed habits due to a fervent desire for God,
if it fends off every thought derived from sense or memory
or troubled disposition, if it is filled, instead, with a new
and lush confusion of reverence and joy, then you can be certain
you are approaching that dear country we call prayer.

* * *

The Holy Spirit has compassion on our weaknesses,
and though we remain impure He often comes to visit us.
When He finds our spirit praying to Him in love,
He immediately dispels the marauding horde of thoughts
that keep it hobbled. And then he bids it forward
to the delicious works of spiritual prayer.

VIII.

No one who loves true prayer and still gives way
to anger or resentment can be protected
from the appearance of insanity.
For he resembles a man who tears at his eyes
in order to see more clearly.

If you long to pray, then stay clear
of all that is opposed to prayer.
In this way, when God draws near
He has only to accompany you.

* * *

Prayer is the rejection of pet speculations.

* * *

A man in chains cannot run; at least he won't
run far. Just so, the mind enslaved to passion
cannot make its way to spiritual prayer.

When the spirit prays purely
without being hindered, the demons
no longer attack from the left, but from the right.

That is, they appear holy, and in a form that flatters
the senses, baiting it to false conceit that it
has attained the aim of prayer.

* * *

When the angel of the Lord arrives,
he scatters by his word alone
every force that acts against us,
and brings to our spirits that light
that shines without deception.

IX.

If you come to know your own measure, you will taste
a sweeter sorrow, and will say, as Isaiah said, *I am
a miserable wretch*. You know you are impure, your very lips
have been defiled, and you stand among a horde
of scheming rebel ingrates. And yet, you dare
to stand before the God of the righteous.

* * *

And even so, if you would pray in truth, you will
suspect a deeper sense of curious confidence.
And a host of angels will walk beside you
showing you the purpose of created things.

Trust this: the holy angels urge us on to prayer. They are ever
with us, rejoicing as they also pray for us. If we, regardless,
remain distracted, we provoke them, given that despite
their efforts to intercede for us we blithely coddle the enemy.

X.

Pray with due reverence, and without anxiety.

* * *

If, so far, you still don't know the grace
of either prayer or psalmody, just press ahead,
and eagerly. You will surely apprehend it.

Take care not to set your heart
on what seems good to you;
rather, work to desire
what is pleasing to God.
In that way, you will be free
from disturbance, and your prayer
will be one of thanksgiving.

* * *

Even as you stand in God's presence,
guard against the demon of unchastity.
He is the most destructive and deceptive
of the bunch, and swifter even
than thought, penetrating the spirit's
watchfulness. He would bid you to believe
your spirit is distracted from God, even
when you stand in His presence
with all due reverence and fear.

XI.

Endure painful trials, and you will be consoled.
Remain constant in the face of bitterness
and taste the sweetness that will follow.

Cultivate a deep humility, and the malice
of demons will not touch you.

At the time of harsh temptations
trust in the power of short, intense prayer.

Do not, in any way, attempt to shape
some likely image, or visualize some form
at the time of prayer.

* * *

Happy is the spirit who achieves
perfect formlessness in the midst of prayer.

Happy is the spirit who prays without distraction
and discovers ever-increasing desire for God.

Happy is the spirit who is spared the love
of material things and is stripped of all
in the midst of prayer.

Happy is the spirit who forgets
where and who he is
in the midst of prayer.

Happy is the one who thinks himself to be
not better than the soil or clay beneath his feet.

Happy is the one who rejoices in the progress
of all men with the same great joy he knows for his own.

Happy is the one who acknowledges all men as god after God.

* * *

The one who prays perfectly is the one
who draws forth his best for God.

XII.

Here's something you can count on: Soon as you provide
some good thing for a stranger, another will come along
and do you wrong. This is—trust me—the enemy's
calculation to make you respond to the injustice
by doing injury to another, or failing to continue
doing good. Sure, you can respond as poorly
as you wish. Just know this: you will utterly
scatter all that you have so carefully gathered up,
and will give the demons precisely what
they hoped to see.

* * *

Don't avoid those who might give you a good beating.
Sure, they'll kick you around, stretch you out, smack you
good and hard—precisely the way the washman cleans
    your clothes.

* * *

Reject neither poverty nor affliction;
they are essential materials
for your constructing
the edifice of prayer.

* * *

To the extent that you continue to give attention
to amenities of comfort, you have not yet glimpsed
the place of prayer, and the joy to be found
in the way of prayer is still a long ways off.

XIII.
When you give your full attention to prayer,
you will find it. Nothing is so sure to follow the path
laid out by one's genuine attention than one's prayer.

Of all the virtues, prayer is most divine.

When you give yourself wholly to prayer, see
that you rise above every other joy.
That is where you will discover
the holy communion that you seek.

Saint Denys the Areopagite
(c. 440–c. 530)

Perhaps better known as Pseudo-Dionysios, this Saint Denys is presumed to have been a Syrian monk, writing under the name of a martyred saint who had heard Saint Paul preach on Mars Hill some four hundred years earlier. His writings are nonetheless revered for their pairing of unmatched philosophical sophistication with a mystical, apophatic vision of God's being beyond comprehension and beyond naming, all of which is made moot by God's inexplicable love for all.

✑ As Beauty Bids

Beauty bids all things come
    to itself (and thus
        we call it beauty).
Just so, it gathers
    all things trembling
        fully to itself.
We speak of it as beauty
    since it is
        the all-comely,
and also tenders
    a compelling glimpse
        of Beauty-Beyond-All.

∾ Beckoning Beauty

It is forever so—
   unvarying, unchanging—
      beautiful but not
as something
   coming into birth
      or falling into death,
and not as what
   might grow or might
      decay, nor is it
beautiful *now* and otherwise *then*.
   It is in itself and of itself
      the uniquely and eternally
beautiful, and the great creating
   cause that beckons
      all creation, and holds
all things in the pulse
   of its existence,
      bears them, keeps them
by the longing within them
   to share in what it is—which is
      to say, to share in what is beautiful.

⤳ As No Other Being

No. This Endless One we wish
        to know looms ever
                at an absolute remove
from every pet conjecture,
        all conception, each limit,
                and thought. And yet,
since that One remains
        the underpinning
                of all that is good,
and by merely being
        is the utter cause
                of everything, to utter praise
to this Beneficence, you
        must turn once more
                to all creation.
He bides there, at the center
        of everything, and everything
                has Him as its destiny.
Suspecting this, the puzzling
        theologians praise Him
                by every name—and also
as the Nameless One.

◌ﾟ *Paradoxical Love in Revelation*

On the one hand, we'd be foolhardy to apply
        words or figures of our own invention
to the hidden, unknowable God.
        And, on the other grasping hand,
His Goodness is not wholly unsuspected.

Of His own He offers us a steady,
        sublime ray, granting actual illumination
to each being according to its modest capacity,
        and with that ray draws every reconciled *nous*
ever upward to the desired contemplation,
        to participation, and to becoming like Him.

To those who fall away His is the still voice calling,
        "Come back!" and His is the power that raises
them again, enabling their willing return.

✑ No Separation

What you see is truly
    the image of *what is so*,
even if *what is so* remains
    for the most part unavailable.

In times to come, don't go
    thinking that the God
will—however justly—
    separate Himself
from those who choose evil;
    instead, it is they who will
separate themselves from Him.

Indeed, already we see
    some united here and now
with Him, loving truth, having
    forsaken selfish passions
in favor of a surpassing desire.

In this life, they already live
    as in the next, attending
to the One, serving as his messengers.

Saint Dorotheos of Gaza
(c. 490–c. 560)

Born to a wealthy family in Antioch, Saint Dorotheos was much loved for his homilies. Equipped with a classical education and a love of books, he became a monk. Later, as founding abbot of a monastery, the saint wrote spiritual instructions for his disciples, praising humility above all other virtues. His works come to us largely through quotations in the writings of Theodore the Studite and his disciples.

∾ Where We Are

We should probably pause,
and discover where we stand and if
we at least stand facing
the most likely direction.
Have we yet left our
fallen city, have we so much
as exited the gate? Have we
cleared the city's spanning
wreck only to languish
among its rubbish heaps?
Have we made a little
progress, or something more?
Have we progressed
so much as halfway
on our journey,
or just a mile or two?
Have you, like me,
advanced, say, several

miles, and then retraced
the same distance in reverse?
Have we come so far
as the Holy City itself,
the City of Peace?
Have we entered its open
gate, or do we stand
cowering outside, unable
to enter into it?

∾ Visitation

My heart was lead, and my mind
was murk. Nothing proved a comfort,
and I remained for that wretched season
shut in on all sides, stifled, gasping for breath.

Regardless, the grace of God arrives
rushing to the soul when its endurance
is exhausted. Of a dreary morning, I
stood gazing round the courtyard, pleading

God for assistance; suddenly I turned
toward the broad katholikón and saw
one dressed as though a bishop enter
the open doors, as though borne on wings.

Within the nave, he remained standing for some time,
his arms raised in prayer. I stood all that while

there behind him in great fear, trembling in prayer,
for I was very alarmed at the sight of him.

When his prayers were spoken, he turned
and walked to me, with each step vanquishing
incrementally my pain and dread. And then
he stood before me and, stretching out his hand,

touched me on the chest and tapped my tender
breastbone saying aloud:
    I waited, I waited for the Lord
    And he stooped down to me.
    He heard my cry.
    He drew me from the deadly pit,
        from the mire and clay.
    He set my feet upon a rock
        and made my footsteps firm.
    He put a new song into my mouth,
        new praise of our God.

He spoke these lines three times, tapping
me each time on the tender breastbone. Then,
he turned and was gone, and instantly, light
flooded my mind, and joy split my heart
with an awful, aching sweetness.

Saint John of the Ladder
(c. 579–649)

*Saint John of the Ladder was born in Syria and entered the monastery at
the age of sixteen. After the death of his spiritual father, Martyrius John,
the saint withdrew to a hermitage, where he lived for some twenty years,
studying the lives of the saints. When he was seventy-five, the monks of Sinai
persuaded him return to serve as their abbot. Four years later he resigned
his charge and returned to his hermitage to prepare for death. His* Ladder
of Divine Ascent *is beloved as a vision of the human struggle to partake of
God's unending Life.*

ᴄᴏ *Prayer*

By its very nature, prayer
avails both our conversation
and our union with the God.

Its sure effect is (notice now!) to hold
the world together. Prayer
is both the mother and the daughter

of our tears, and occasions
expiation of all sin. It is a bridge
across temptation and a wall

against affliction, both a future
joy and present act, endlessly
opening to a flood of graces.

ᴥ *Purpose and Order*

Keep it simple—your prayer—and bear in mind
how the publican and the prodigal each
were reconciled to God by a single plea.
Such a simple lifting of the heart—a plea
in prayer—is the same for all, though we
observe many sorts of prayer and many forms.

Some pray as to a friend, and some
as to a master. Some lift their praises
and heartfelt petitions less for themselves
than for others. Some seek spiritual
treasures, or glory, or some greater
reassurance in their prayers. Some beg
to be released entirely from the enemy,
and some to be relieved of debt.

Whatever your purpose, know that thanksgiving
should hold first place in our rule of prayer.
Next should come confession, and genuine
contrition of the soul. Only when these
have been accomplished might
our several bold petitions find a voice.
This approach to prayer is far superior—
or so one of the brothers was told
most recently by an angel of the Lord.

If You Would Prevail

While we languish yet in prison, let us attend
to him who told an ill-clad Peter to adopt
the garment of obedience, to shed
his own poor wishes, and, having been
stripped of them, to approach the Lord
in prayer, seeking only His great desire.
Then, poor pilgrim, will you receive the God,
Who takes the helm of your very soul,
and pilots you surely. Following
an extended time of prayer, do not say
that nothing has been gained, for you
have already acquired something, no?
What, after all, appears a greater good
than to cling to the Lord, and to continue
in unceasing union with Him?

Prepare for your set time of formal prayer
with an unceasing plea of mercy in your heart.
In this way, you will make quick progress.
I have witnessed how some—outstanding
in just such obedience—suffered far
as possible throughout the day to bear
in mind the thought of God. They wept,
shuddering, as soon as they stood to keep
their rule of prayer.

Never refuse a request to pray for the soul
of another, even when you suspect yourself
to have lost the gift of prayer, for often the faith
of the person making the request will evoke
the sweet contrition of the one who is asked
to offer prayer. Thereafter, reject whatever pride
arrives when your prayer for the other has been heard;
the agency of grace lay in their faith and not your own.

Whatever is obtained in long, persistent prayer
will not leave us. When one has met the Lord
in prayer, he has no need for words; the Spirit Himself
intercedes for him with deep groaning, full,
unutterable. Shape no image during prayer, for this
will bring distraction. If you would pray, and truly,
let mercy be foremost. When fire comes to warm the heart,
it brings prayer's resurrection; and look! when prayer
is thus revived it flies to heaven, and sends down
a holy light and fire to the upper chamber of the soul.

Just as, once mounted, a good horse warms
and quickens its pace, the soul proceeds
towards prayer. Worse than taking away
the water cup from the lips of one who thirsts
is our dragging from its utterance the soul
before it has attained its long desired prayer.

Do not quit prayer so long as, by His grace, the fire and the water remain, for it may be that in all your life no such moment will ever come again—this moment when your very soul asks mercy for your sins.

The end of prayer is to be snatched away to God.

Saint Isaac of Nineveh
(† 700)

The saint was born in the region of Qatar on the Persian Gulf's western shore. When he and his brother were very young, the two entered a monastery together. As much for his compassion as for his asceticism, his fame as a holy man and teacher spread widely during his lifetime. He was subsequently ordained bishop of Nineveh, the former capital of Assyria to the north, but asked to abdicate after only five months. He then went south to the wilderness of Mount Matout, where he lived in solitude for many years, studying the Scriptures and composing his Ascetical Homilies, *which have given consolation and guidance to generations of monastics and others pursuing lives of prayer.*

∾ Love's Purpose

In love did He bring the world
     into being, and in love
        does He guide its difficult,
slow-seeming journey now
     through the arc of time. In love will He
        one day bring all the world to a wondrous,
transformed state, and utterly
     in love will it be taken wholly up
        into the great mystery of the One
who has performed these things—and all of this so that
     in love absolutely will the course
        and form and governance of all creation
at long last be comprised.

∽ The Measure of His Mercy

As a grip of sand is
    flung into the sea,
so do the sins of all flesh
    enter the mind of God.

Just as the strength of a flowing spring
    is not hindered by a handful of earth,
so the compassion of the Creator is not daunted
    by the wickedness of His creatures.

Know this: whoever bears a grudge when he prays
    is like a man who sows grain in the sea
    and expects to reap a harvest.
Regardless, just as the fire's flames
    cannot be prevented from reaching upwards,
so the prayers of the compassionate
    will not be kept from their ascent.

∽ The Merciful Heart

The heart's pulsing ache—oh to have
    that same heart's burning
        for persons, for birds, all manner
of animal, and even for the demons.

At the remembrance
        and at the sight of all such creatures,
                the merciful man's eyes
fill with tears which rise with a great, increasing

compassion that wells
        and urges his heart,
                so that it grows ever
more tender and cannot endure any

harm or slightest sorrow
        for anything found
                in creation. Such a man
is ceaseless in tear-attended prayer,

even now, and even for
        irrational animals,
                and for enemies of truth,
and for all who harm it, that they may be both
        guarded and forgiven.

∾ Mystery Beyond the Words

Even if such words as *wrath*, *anger*,
hatred, and many meager others
are pressed into speaking of the Creator,
we should not suppose that He
ever does anything in anger or hatred
or zeal. Many such figures are employed
in the roiling span of Scripture, provisional
terms far removed from Who He Is.

Even as our own, relatively rational persons
have already been tweaked, increasingly
if slowly made more competent in holy
understanding of the Mystery—namely, that we
should not take things quite so literally,
but should suspect (concealed within
the corporal surfaces of unlikely narrative)
a hidden providence and eternal knowledge
guiding all—so too we shall in future
come to see the sweep of many things
to be quite contrary to what our current,
puerile processes afford us.

∾ *Gehenna, Its Duration*

Even in the matter of afflictions
      —the judgment of Gehenna, say—
there bides a hidden mystery, whereby
      the Maker has taken as a starting point
our patent willfulness, using even Hell
      as a way of bringing to perfection
His greater dispensation.

If the world to come proves entirely the realm
      of mercy, love, and goodness,
how then a final state that claims
      requital for its measure?

That we should think that hell
      is not also full
of love and mingled with compassion
      would be an insult to our God.
By saying He will deliver us
      to suffering without purpose, we
most surely sin. We blaspheme also if we say
      that He will act with spite or with a vengeful purpose,
as if He had a need to avenge Himself.

⟋⟍ Awaiting Us at Last

I am of the opinion
        that the God shall of a radiant morning make
full manifest a chaste, surpassing outcome,
        a matter of immense, immeasurable
compassion on the part

of the loving Creator,
        even with respect to this difficult matter
of suffering, that out of it—even of
        Gehenna's bleak, abysmal torment—the infinite
wealth of His love we

will behold all the more,
        and bountifully. Among all His actions,
there is none that is not entirely
        a matter of mercy, love, and compassion:
these comprise the beginning
        and the luminous end of His dealings with us.

Saint Francis of Assisi
(c. 1182–1226)

*Born to a wealthy family in Assisi, the saint showed early on that he had
no interest in either commerce or the wealth it brought, but had great
compassion and charity for those who suffered, most notably lepers of the
Lazar Houses near his hometown. In time, having renounced both family
and wealth, he founded the order of friars now bearing his name; not long
thereafter, he received Saint Clare and other chaste women as a nearby
sister order.*

*Two years before his death, in the midst of a Lenten fast, Saint Francis
received what would later be called* stigmata, *the sign of his having identi-
fied with the sufferings of Christ.*

༰ Mercy

This is how our Lord allowed me
to begin my healing: While I yet walked
in sin, the mere sight of lepers was as
a bitterness I could not bear. Therefore,
the Lord Himself drew me to life
among them, and so doing gave me
to have mercy on them. By the time
I left them, the bitterness had turned
to a sweetness of soul and of body.

Thereafter, I lingered a little while
in the world, then left it altogether.
In the holy churches, the Lord granted me
such overwhelming faith that my whole
prayer—and my sole manner of speech—
was to say: *Lord Jesus Christ, we adore you!*

In all Your churches the whole world wide
we announce your blessing, for through
Your holy cross you have reconciled the world.

∽ The Reach to Speak His Name

Holy Lord, and only.
Sole strength and greatness
singular. You ascend supremely,
O almighty King. Progenitor
and Sovereign of the heavens
and the earth, both Three and One,
Lord God of all the holy ones.
All good, sole good, and highest
good, our true and living Master.
Love and lover manifest.
Wisdom and the wise.
The humble and the patient,
Beauty beckoning. Gentle shelter.
The peace and joy and hope of all.
Just and moderate, you are our
treasure, all sufficient. Protector
and the shield of our souls.
Our life-preserving food and our
cool drink. Our only hope, our faith,
our love. All our sweetness falls
from You, who give eternal life.
Exceeding mystery, Master,
God omnipotent. Savior merciful.

✒ *His Blessings and His Praise*

To You belong all praises, all honor
and every blessing, though no man
is worthy to so much as speak
Your name. We praise You in the face
of every creature—most especially
Brother Sun who spans our days,
by whom You give us light. His splendor,
radiant and beautiful, bears Your likeness.
You are praised through Sister Moon
and all attendant stars. In their beauty
and clear light we see Your hand.
You are praised through Brother Wind
and through the skies, the cloud-filled
and the calm, and You are praised
through every shade of weather
by which You feed your creatures.
You are praised through Sister Water,
who is willing, modest, precious, and chaste.
You are praised through Brother Fire
by whom you trouble the night; for he
is beautiful, playful, robust, and strong.
You are praised through our Sister Mother Earth,
who feeds and nurtures us, who offers
luscious fruits bearing colored flowers and herbs.
You are praised through those who show mercy
for the love of You, who suffer infirmity
and manifold difficulties with unabated love.

Blessed are all who endure all this in peace,
for You will mark their endurance with a crown.
You are praised through our Sister Bodily Death,
whom no one living can escape. Grief to those
who meet her unrelieved of mortal sin.
Blessed are those whom death will discover
in the midst of Your most holy will, for no
second death shall ever harm them.
All people, praise and bless my Lord, and give
Him thanks, serve Him with deep humility.

Saint Clare of Assisi
(c. 1193–1254)

*The eldest daughter of a Count, the saint heard Saint Francis preaching
in the streets of Assisi and was convicted by his words. In 1212, Clare
and her sister Agnes fled their home to follow Francis, who received
them into religious life. The two made vows of poverty, chastity, and
obedience, and stayed with Benedictine nuns until moving to San
Damiano, where Saints Clare and Agnes founded the Order of Poor.
Saint Clare served as abbess of the community until her death.*

✑ *The Depth of His Touch*

When you have loved Him,
you shall be chaste.
When you have touched Him,

you shall be pure.
When you have received Him,
you shall be a virgin.
He is the One Whose power is stronger,
Whose generosity is more abundant,
Whose appearance more beautiful,
Whose love more tender,
Whose courtesy more gracious, and in
Whose embrace you are already caught up.
Have you noticed?
He has laid precious stones upon your breast,
has pressed precious pearls to your ears,
and has surrounded you with luminous gems
as though with gleaming blossoms of springtime,
and see! He has set upon your head a golden crown
as a sign announcing your holiness.

∽ The One Thing Necessary

One thing alone is necessary, one alone
is needful. And of that singular treasure I bear
witness, and toward it I now encourage you—
and all of this for love of Him to Whom
you offer yourself as a holy, pleasing sacrifice.

What you now hold, may you always and forever hold.
What you do, may you forever do, and never abandon,
but with a quickened and a quickening pace, light step,

and unswerving feet, proceed—surely, full of joy,
and with great speed.

Offer your vows to the Most High in eager pursuit
of that perfection to which the Spirit of the Lord has called you.

⤳ *Paradox and Promise*

Look upon Him Who became
contemptible for you, and—if you choose—
follow His way, becoming contemptible
to the world, so long as you do so for Him.

More lovely than all things, He
became the lowest, despised, struck,
scourged countless times and raked
across His perfect Body. And then, amid
the sufferings of the horrid Cross, He died. For you.

If you suffer with Him, you shall reign with Him.
Weep with Him and you shall rejoice with Him.
Die with Him upon the cross of wretchedness, and life is yours,
and, yes, your dwelling forever in Him.

Blesséd Angela of Foligno
(c. 1248–1309)

Born in Foligno, Italy, Blessed Angela is reputed to have been self-indulgent in her early life. She married young, and was widowed some years later. At that time she experienced what she characterized as a conversion, and joined the Third Order of Saint Francis. At the request of her confessor, Friar Arnold, Angela dictated to him an account of her mystical visions and ecstasies.

⸙ *His Entry and Delight*

Unfailingly I knew that it was Christ
who warmed me, for nothing sets the soul ablaze
as when Christ has entered it and charms it
with His love. Such a heat and flame is not
the fire with which the soul is sometimes
set ablaze but is a roar of sweet and gentle love.
When this happens, all the members
apprehend a strange disjointing, and still
I wish it to be so. Such is the extreme delight
that I feel I would want always to remain
in just this state, aching as my body fills
with Him. And if I hear the bones
both crack and moan at this disjointing,
I hear it all the more when the Holy Mysteries
are raised in consecration. It is especially then
that my hands suffer this disjointing and (see?) are opened.

༄ A Vision

I saw a fullness, and a singeing
       brightness with which I then
              felt myself to be so filled
that words now fail to serve,
       nor can I reach sufficiently
              to find a meet comparison.

I would not say I saw a bodily form,
       but He was as He is in heaven,
              which is to say of such exquisite
beauty that I have no means
       to speak it, save to say
              He is the Beauty, the All Good.

༄ Divine Light

No one can be saved
       without divine light.
Divine light causes us
       to begin and thereafter
enables our progress
       as it leads us
to the summit of perfection.

Therefore, if you desire
    to begin
and would receive
    this divine light, pray.

If you have begun to make
    some little progress
and would see this light
    intensified within you, pray.

And if you have reached
    the summit of perfection,
and desire to be super-illumined
    so as to remain in that state, pray.

His Blazing Embrace

The embrace of God puts fire to the soul,
by which the soul entire is felt to burn
for Christ, accompanied by light so great the soul
suspects the immensity of God's appalling goodness.
You won't get used to it, nor will you know its scope.
The effect of this fire within the soul is to render it
certain and secure that Christ is there within it.

And still, what we have said is nothing
compared to what you find in the embrace of God.

∽ The Darkness

When I enter that darkness I cannot
recall a bit about anything human,
or about the God-man, or anything
owning specific form. Nonetheless,
I see all and I see nothing. As this
that I have spoken of withdraws—though
not completely, as it seems to stay
with me—I see the God-man. He draws
my soul with utmost gentleness
and maybe He whispers *You are I
and I am you.* I see, then, those eyes
and that face so gracious and attractive
as He leans to draw me to Himself.
In short, what proceeds from those eyes
and what descends from that face is what
I said I saw in that previous darkness rising
from within, and which delights me so
that I can say nothing much about it.
When I am in the God-man, then my soul
is alive. And I am in the God-man
much more than in the other vision
of seeing God with darkness. The soul
comes alive in that vision of the God-man.
Even so, the vision with darkness draws me
so much more that there is no comparison.
On the other hand, I am in the God-man
almost continually. It began to be this way

when, of a moment, I was given profound
assurance that there was no intermediary
between God and myself. Since that moment,
I have not known a day or a night in which
I did not continually experience this joy,
this pulse within the humanity of Christ.

∽ His Doing

God is the One who draws me, and God
the One who lifts me to that place.
I could not approach it on my own,
for by myself I would not know
so much as how to desire it, how
to seek it. As it is, I am now almost
continually drawn. And if I'm not,
then God will often raise me to it
with no need, apparently, for my consent.
When I expect it least, suddenly my soul
is raised by God and in Him even I
hold dominion, and even I comprehend
the whole world. It seems, then, as if I am
no longer bound on earth but utterly
in heaven, and utterly in God.

Saint Nicephorus the Hesychast
(c. 1250–1280)

Born a Catholic, the saint later became Orthodox and thereafter lived in asceticism on Mount Athos as a monk. He was a spiritual father of Saint Gregory Palamás, and, in strong desire to share his experiences with his brothers, he wrote a work on noetic prayer, counseling that a life of unceasing prayer is not only possible, but is the only way truly to partake of life in Christ.

∾ *Reunion*

You know already that the breath
moves in and out in order to infuse
the heart with the air it craves;
as I have said, then, recollect
your mind, and draw it—and *yes,*
I am speaking of your mind—
as if you drew it *in*
through your very nostrils.
Attend to its descent, as it finds
the path to reach the heart. Drive it then,
and force it downward with the very
air you breathe to enter with a rush into
that famished, pulsing chamber.

When it arrives, you will taste
the joy that follows. You'll have nothing
to regret. Just as a man who has been far
from home a long time cannot restrain

his delight at seeing his wife and children—
just so, the spirit overflows with joy
and with unspeakable delight when it is
once more united with the soul.

New Knowledge

Thereafter, you must see to it
that so long as your spirit bides
—that is, at home within the heart—
you must not stay silent nor idle,
you must not take this treasure lightly.
Have no other occupation, no other
meditation than the cry
of *Lord Jesus Christ, Son of God,*
have mercy on me!
Under no condition acquiesce
to rest, but fix your heart solely
on this elevating work.

This practice will protect your spirit
from wandering, and will make it
impregnable, wholly inaccessible
to the deceptions of the enemy.

The prayer will draw you every day
more deeply into love, more fully
into love *with* and in desire *for* your God.

Mechthild of Magdeburg
(c. 1260–1282/94)

She is said to have experienced her first mystical visions at the age of twelve, when—as she herself writes—she was "greeted by the Holy Ghost." From that day, this greeting came to be her daily joy. Identifying with the suffering of Christ, she desired to be despised by all undeservedly; to this end, she left her home to become a Beguine. Here, under the spiritual guidance of the Dominicans, she led a life of prayer.

ᴗ Love's Four Things

Love—the genuine and pure—holds four
essential elements that never rest:
increasing desire,
a suffering that flows, now streaming,
a sense of burning in both soul and body,
and ceaseless union with the One Great Vigilance.

These are unavailable, save to those
who lean fully into full exchange with God.
Thereby, give to God everything that is yours,
within and without, and He will give
you everything that is His.

When the hour of bliss has passed, and God
has given his most sublime consolation
to the soul in love, even then, the belovéd
is so utterly content that she considers
all things good, even that
which the estranged soul feels as pain.

∽ God's Splendor Reflected

You ask me to continue with these words,
but I cannot. Bliss, glory, brightness, eros, truth:
these things so overwhelm that I turn mute, unable
to speak anything more of what I know. And still,
there's this: A mirror is set in heaven
before the breast of each embodied soul.
In it shines the image of the Holy Trinity,
giving truth and knowledge of every virtue
the body ever practiced and of all
the gifts the soul has met on earth.

And in that wrenching confrontation, the glorious
reflection of every person shines forth, and turns
again into the sublime majesty from which
it first flowed out. And look! the angels' radiance
is now a fire, burnished with love, for they take
great delight in our blessedness. They serve us so,
and effortlessly, and their reward increases
so long as earth exists.

True love of God bears the same power in angels
that it does in us, though our willingness to serve
requires effort, due to our being hobbled by our sin.

How We Become Like God

To the extent the we love mercy and we keep
unfailing watch, we are like our Father in Heaven,
who ceaselessly performs these things in us.

To the extent that we suffer poverty, humiliation,
rejection and pain, we are like the Son of God,
who endured and tolerated all such suffering.

To the extent that we flow outward with the full
abundance of our hearts, and give our complete substance
to the poor, and spend our lives in service to sick, we
are like the Holy Spirit who is made manifest
as the abundant outpouring of the Father and the Son.

Gertrude of Helfta
(1256–c. 1302)

Little, if anything, is known about this mystic's family or her birth.
At the age of five, however, she began her studies at the Benedictine
monastery in Helfta. As a teen, she became a nun, continuing her liberal
studies. Early in her twenties, she had a mystical experience that drew
her from secular studies to the Scriptures and theology. To assist her
sisters, she wrote simpler versions of difficult scriptural passages, and
compiled collections of the sayings of the saints. She served as spiritual
mother to her fellow nuns and—through correspondence—with many
others outside the monastery.

✑ Prayer and Pleading

Even during worship she puzzled
over certain odd appearances.
And while she was thus occupied,
she forgot the several sore petitions
she had made, neglecting to observe
if any had been answered. Even so,
in due time, she was aware that He Himself
had found peaceful, efficacious biding
in the hearts and souls of those
of her community she previously
had glimpsed in mystic elevation, cherishing
their nearness to the God. And then
she brought to mind a certain one
who'd asked for prayer, and so
she prayed. The Lord Himself responded.

No one can make the ascent of faith I've shown you
who is not raised by confidence; and the one
for whom you pray is lacking it. She answered,
Lord, it seems to me that this lack of confidence
proceeds from deep humility, which most times
You reward with ever more abundant grace.
He answered in compassion, *I will come down.*
I will communicate my gifts to her, and to every soul
who walks the peaceful valley of humility.

⤫ Of Humility and Worthiness

As she approached the cup one day
in order to partake of these, the holy
and life-bestowing Mysteries, and while
the sweet, antiphonal refrain—*Rejoice*
and be glad!—was being sung, she heard
"Holy, holy, holy," and immediately fell
into prostration, low to the ground
with deep, heartfelt humility. And doing so
she prayed to Him that He would make her
worthy to receive this His heavenly feast
prepared for the glory and welfare of all.

At her petition, the Son of God—suddenly
bending to her as a sweetest lover—pressed
upon her soul His sweetest kiss. And as
the second "Holy" was then intoned,

He said, *Behold, within this kiss, and with*
this second "Holy" addressed to me, I impart
all holiness of My divinity and My humanity,
that you may be worthily prepared
to take these Holy Mysteries to your lips.

ᘓ At Vespers

And while the others sang *I saw waters flowing,*
the Lord inclined to speak to her: *Behold*
My heart: henceforth it is yours, your temple.
Now search among the other regions of My body
and take for yourself other rooms in which to make
monastic life: from this day on, My body is your cloister.
She answered, "Lord, I know no way
to seek farther or to choose, for I find
such delicious plenty in Your sweetest heart
which You have named my temple.
Apart from it I find no rest, nor refreshment,
things necessary in a cloister."
He said, *If it pleases you, both of these are waiting*
in My heart; and some, like Dominic, never left
the temple, both eating and sleeping there. Still,
do choose; some other rooms you may find
useful to include as efficacious cloister.
At His bidding, she took His feet for her ambulatory,
His hands for her working place. His mouth became
her parlor, His eyes her library. His ears she chose

as her confessional, to which He bid her go
after any fall, so as ascending the five steps
of humiliation—I am a wretch, a sinner, a beggar,
evil, and unworthy—she might always turn
ever and again to the overflowing abyss of His mercy.

Meister Eckhart
(c. 1260–1327)

*Born near Erfurt in Thuringia, Eckhart became Professor of Theology,
taking a leading pastoral role in the Dominican Order. He makes use
of familiar religious language, but presents his mystical vision in freshly
vivid terms. Through such imagery—the Eucharist as a spark of the soul,
the divine Abyss, the birth of the Word within the heart—the mystic
encourages those who desire noetic prayer to press ahead to that which
lies beyond such images.*

∽ The Prayer of a Heart Detached

What is the prayer of a heart grown calm
        in the peace of God?
From such a purity one no longer prays
        as we are wont to pray.
From such a purity one is free from asking
        any further gift of God, and is free
        also from asking that anything
        be taken away.

A heart in calm detachment asks
for nothing, nor has anything
it would wish to shed.
Its prayer is finally only for uniformity
with God. This is its entire prayer.

∽ *Unburdened*

And that is why I think it far
better than anything that a man
should abandon himself wholly to God,
whatever it may be that God desires
to impose on him—contempt or heavy labor
or any manner of hardship—so long
as he accepts it joyfully, in gratitude,
and gives himself to be led solely by God.
Just so, if you tilt your head to learn from God
and gladly, and thereby follow Him,
all will be well with you.
With such a disposition, you
can easily accept honors and ease.
Should hardships and disgrace arrive,
you will bear them also, and be
oddly pleased to bear them.

∾ *Beyond Sorrows*

With trust in God and faith, a man
      might finally see the God to be so good
           that no sorrow or harm can come to him
unless it be a remedy for greater sorrow, greater harm;
      unless it offer him an ever greater consolation;
           unless, with it, a greater thing is made, revealing
all the more God's love. With such an understanding,
      a man might give his will wholly to the will of God,
           so that the two are one, united in a single will—
and so much so that the man will see that even
      harm, even damnation bides as the means by which
           God's greater good is realized.

∾ *The One Image*

This is why the teachers say
      that the blessed in heaven perceive
      creatures free from every creaturely image,
      and that they perceive them
      in that one Image which is God,
      and in which God knows
      and loves, and wills Himself
      and wills all things.
And this is what God Himself teaches
      us to pray and to desire, when we say,
      Our Father . . . hallowed be Your name,

which is to say, *Let us know You alone.*
And more, *Your kingdom come*, which is to say,
that I may possess nothing but You,
my only treasure.

Saint Gregory Palamás
(1296–1359)

*Having turned away from the imperial favor that was his birthright
in Constantinople, the saint was drawn to Mount Athos to become a
monk. In time, he was granted permission to live as a hermit, pursuing
unceasing prayer. He served as Archbishop of Thessaloniki, but is best
remembered for having successfully defended this hesychastic practice
against those who would deny its value. He is said to have seen "the
Uncreated Light."*

✑ Uncreated Light

This light of which I speak is not
the essence of God—not likely—for His essence
is not to be seen, not to be considered.

Nor is this light an angel, for it bears
—without question—the Master's face.
On occasion, it draws a man out from the body,

or else—and better—even without drawing him
from the flesh, lifts him to ineffable heights.
At other times it alters the body itself,

and communicates its own splendor to it
when—a wonder!—the light that deifies
the simple flesh condescends to light the eye.

Thus indeed did the great Arsenios appear
when caught in prayer of silent struggle,
and also Stephen, crushed by stones,

and thus, our father Moses newly come down
from the holy mountain, radiant. More than this,
sometimes the light "speaks" clearly,

as it were, with ineffable words, to the one
who leans into it in contemplation. Such
was the case with Paul. Moreover, Gregory

the Theologian, has told us, "It condescends
from elevated places where it dwells, so that He
who in His own nature from eternity

is neither seen nor held by any being may be
in modest measure glimpsed by a created nature."
The one who has received this light, by studying, say,

himself-thus-illumined, will thereafter perceive
in his very *nous* that same substance, which
the children touched as *manna*, the holy bread come down.

To the Summit of Tabor

When the saints lean in to contemplate
the uncreated light grown luminous
in themselves—and seeing it by divine
and deifying union of the Spirit,
through the full mysterious agency
of Her illuminations—*then* they see
the very garment of their ongoing change.

Their *nous* becomes both glorified and filled
by beauty of the Word, a beauty beyond measure
and a splendor. Just so, on Mount Tabor,
the divinity of the Word glorified
with divine light the body joined to it—
for the glory that the Father gave Him,
He Himself now gives to those
whose obedience has led them to approach
this very summit, drawn to radiant life.

Effort and Study

We have said that wisdom comes to man
through effort and through study—not
that it is *only* effort and study, but that it is
seldom unattended by these. The Lord
dwells in men variously according
to the way of those who seek Him.

He appears in one way to an active man,
in another to a contemplative, another yet
to the man of vision, and still another
to the zealous or to those already deified.
Divine vision arrives in countless ways, just
as Divinity is not to be reduced to singularity.
Among the prophets, some have seen the God
in dreams, and others when awake, by means
of paradox and mirror. To Moses He was shown,
appearing face to face, without the veil
of these our troubled terms.

Richard Rolle of Hampole
(1300–1349)

The mystic was raised near Pickering, and studied briefly at Oxford. He remains a revered religious writer—composing in both English and Latin, a Bible translator, and a hermit. After many years as a wandering pilgrim, he spent his final years at Hampole, near the Cistercian convent there. After his death, he was regarded by many as a saint, but was never canonized.

∽ *God's Love*

O Holy Spirit, Who breathes
where You will, breathe into me
and draw me to Yourself.

Invest the nature You have shaped,
with gifts so flowing with honey that,
from intense joy in Your sweetness,

this clay might turn from lesser things,
that it may accept (as You give them)
spiritual gifts, and through pleasing

jubilation, it may melt, entirely,
in holy love, reaching finally out
to touch the Uncreated Light.

✒ *Invitation to the God*

Sear my inmost being
with Your fire, and my heart
will burn on Your altar forever.

Come, I beg You, O sweet
and true glory! Come, O most
desired sweetness! Come,

my Beloved, Who are my whole
consolation, to my soul—now languishing
for Your sake and inclined to You—

and slip into it with most
sweetly flowing love. Set ablaze
with Your heat every penetrable

place of my heart and, by filling
its inmost places with Your light,
feed the whole with the honey-flowing

joy of Your love, in order
to snatch up in new, noetic
union this mind and body.

~ *Love's Effect*

Love, moreover,
does not suffer
the loving soul
to continue apart,
exiled inside itself.

Rather, love carries
that soul beyond
itself and nearer
the Beloved,
so that the soul
would rather
be there, joined
to that it loves,
than where the body
(which depends
on it for feeling
and for life) languishes.

Julian of Norwich
(1342–c.1423)

An English mystic and visionary, Julian is best known as the author—or, more accurately, the recipient—of Sixteen Shewings of Divine Love *in her thirtieth year. She is thought to have been a Benedictine nun, living as an anchorite. According to these revelations, the overriding impulse of God toward humankind is unqualified love, and her compelling vision of "the restoration of all things in God's love" puts her in laudable company.*

∽ *His Suffering Love*

Then said Jesus, our kind Lord: *If you*
    are pleased, then I am pleased:
        it is a joy, a bliss, an endless satisfying to Me
that ever I suffered passion for thee; and if
        I might suffer more, surely, I would suffer more.

In this my understanding
    was lifted up to Heaven, and there
        I saw three heavens: and at these
I marveled greatly. And though I saw
    three heavens—and all in the blesséd
        manhood of Christ—none is more, none
is less, none is higher, none is lower,
    but all are commensurate in bliss.

For the First Heaven, Christ
    revealed His Father; in no bodily likeness,
        but in His property and in His working.

That is to say, I saw in Christ
        that the Father *is*, and that the working
            of the Father appears just so: He gives
reward to His Son, Jesus Christ. This gift
        and this reward is of such bliss to Jesus
            that there is no greater boon that would
have pleased Him better. The First
        Heaven—that is, the pleasing of the Father—
            was revealed to me as one heaven; and it was
full and blissful: for He is full pleased
        with all the deeds that Jesus has done
            in securing our salvation. Wherefore we become—
not only His by purchase, but also
        by the courteous gift of His Father we
            become—and we become His bliss, His right reward,
His worship, and His crown. (And this
        was a singular marvel, a delectable
            beholding, that we become His crown!) This
that I say is such great bliss to Jesus that He sets
        as nothing all His travail, and His hard Passion,
            and His cruel and shameful death.
And in these words: *If that I might suffer more,*
        I would suffer more—I saw in truth
            that as often as He might die, so often He would,
and love should never have let Him rest
        till He had done it.

The God Alone

We know in faith that the God alone
took our nature, and no one but He,
and furthermore, that Christ alone
performed all great works belonging
to our salvation. In this way, He alone
acts now in final restoration. He dwells
here in us. He measures us, and cares
throughout this life for us to bring us
to His bliss. And this He will continue
as long as any soul dwells on earth who will
come to Him—so much so that even if
no willing soul remained on earth save one,
He would be with her, with her alone, until
He had brought her to His bliss.

His Comfort

Sin is necessary, said our Lord.
And in that word, that uttered
sin, His voice set wholly
and intact within my mind
the shape of all that is not good
—the shame, contempt,
concupiscent denial of Himself
that He endured for us,

endured both in His life
and in His death, and every pain
of every other creature here, to boot.

For we are all in part
denied, and so we
ought to be, following
our Master, Jesus, full until
we are fully purged—which is
to say, until we have thus utterly
denied our willful flesh
and every áffect and affection
that is not wholly good.

Beholding this, all pain
that ever was and all
that may ever come to be
was shown to me
and quickly turned
into a consolation.
I saw all this, but could
not see, at that point, sin,
for I believe it has no substance,
no share in being, nor can it be
recognized except by the pain
it causes. Still, it seems to me
that pain *is* something—for a time.

It purges us, and makes us
know ourselves, and helps
us ask for mercy. For the Passion
of our Lord is yet our comfort
against all this, and that remains
His blessed will for all who will
be saved. He comforts—readily
and sweetly—with His words,
and says, *All will be well. All
will be well. Every manner
of thing will be well.*

Walter Hilton
(†1396)

Not much is known of his life, except that he was the head of a house of Augustinian Canons at Thurgarton in Nottinghamshire. He was close to the Carthusians, though not a member of the order. His Scala Perfectionis (Ladder of Perfection) is his most telling work. At a time when excesses of reformed theology had succeeded in shifting the popular sense of Christian vocation to being a mere matter of fire insurance (salvation from hell), Walter Hilton's mystical vision and his writings continued to insist that the ancient way—the way of theosis, of union with God—was the Christian's ultimate calling.

◆ The Soul, His Spouse

And all these gracious apprehensions
I call fair words, I call sweet speakings
of our Lord Jesus to the soul, which
He means to make His own true Spouse.
He shows His mysteries, proffers gifts
from His treasury. He arrays the soul
with them full beautifully. She need not
thereafter be ashamed in the company
of her fellows, to appear before the face
of Jesus her Spouse. All this lovely dalliance
of private conference between Jesus and a soul
may be called a hidden word; of the which
the Scripture speaks: *Now there was a word
spoken to me in secret.* Moreover, *to me
there was spoken a secret word, and the veins
of His whispering my ear has perceived.*

What the Light Reveals

After this and by the selfsame light the soul
spiritually sees the beauty of the Angels,
the worthiness of their nature, the subtlety
of their substance, their bright confirmation
in grace, their fullness in endless bliss,
the spanning diversity of their orders;
distinctions of persons, how they all live
in light of endless truth; and how they burn
all in love of the Holy Ghost, according
to the worthiness of their orders;
how they see and love and praise Jesus
in blessed rest without ceasing.

Then begins the soul to have acquaintance
and great fellowship with the blessed spirits.
They are full tender, and they busy about
such a soul to help it, as they are ministers
to teach it. And often by their presence
and touching of their light they drive out fancies
from the soul. They enlighten the soul
graciously; they comfort the soul
with sweet words suddenly sounded
in a clean heart, and if any disease
falls spiritually, they serve that soul
and minister to it all that is needed.
Thus St. Paul said of them: *Don't you know*
that they are all ministering spirits, sent
for them who shall be heirs of salvation?

⮑ Knowledge unto Knowledge, Evermore

The soul is so well pleased beholding
what Angels are and what they do that she
might willingly attend to nothing else;
but nudged by their increasing help the soul
wakes up, seeing all the more; for knowledge
in a clean soul rises high above all creaturely
revelations, which is to behold the blesséd
nature of Jesus Christ Himself. By knowing
the creature the Creator is known. And this
she may do well enough by the light of grace
going before her. She cannot err as long as she
continues in that light. Then is opened truly
to the eye of the soul both the unity in substance,
and distinction of persons in the Blessed Trinity.

Nicholas of Cusa
(1401–1464)

Born in Germany, Nicholas was strongly influenced by the works of Meister Eckhart. He studied in Padua, and after being ordained a Catholic priest, he worked with the Council of Florence, in hopes of assisting in the union of the churches. He was made Cardinal and Bishop of Bressanone. His principal works are De docta ignorantia *(On Scientific Ignorance),* De conjecturis *(On Conjectures), and* De ludo globi *(On the Game of the World).*

∾ *Knowing Nothing*

Our good man Socrates believed he knew
nothing save that he did not know much.
The very wise Solomon declared all things
difficult, complex, not to be explained.
Another wise man of divine spirit insists
that wisdom—the very seat of understanding—
lies hidden "from the eyes of the living."
And likewise, the profound Aristotle,
in the First Philosophy, asserts that—even
with things most apparent in nature—we
encounter the same trouble as a night owl
blinking, straining to look at the sun.

∽ Within the Cloud

In which case, I finally see how
necessary it is to lean into that cloud
and to grin, admitting the coincidence
of opposites, quite aside from all
capacity of reason, and to seek
in that impossible obscurity the truth,
precisely at the point where its apparent
impossibility confronts me most
audaciously. For there, beyond all
reason, and above every bold ascent
—even there, where I glimpse that
which every intellect judges to be
most distant from truth, there
You bide, my God, who remain
our absolute necessity. And look,
the more that cloud is proven both
obscure and patently impossible, the more
truly His necessity shines forth
and the less veiled it appears,
drawing ever more near my puzzlement.

∾ *His Mercy*

I have proposed, Master, by way
of likeness, by crude figures of speech,
a sort of foretaste of Your nature.
For this, You who are ever-merciful, spare me
for attempting to trace the untraceable
savor of Your sweetness. Who am I,
wretched and sinful, to attempt
to show Who cannot be shown,
to make visible Who is invisible,
to offer a taste of Your infinite, utterly
inexpressible sweetness? I have never yet
merited so much as a sip of it myself,
so certainly my words will diminish
rather than magnify this sweetness
I desire, and desire to name. So great
is Your Goodness, even so, that You allow
the blind to speak of the light.

Saint Catherine of Siena
(1347–1380)

The twenty-third of twenty-five children, Saint Catherine received no formal education. At the age of seven, and against her family's wishes, she consecrated her virginity to Christ, and in her eighteenth year she took the habit of the Dominican Tertiaries. Her unusual fasting practice included living for many weeks on nothing but the Blessed Sacrament. In 1366, the saint experienced what she calls a "Mystical Marriage" with Jesus, after which she began to tend the sick and serve the poor. In 1370, she received a series of mystical visions of the afterlife.

⁓ Waking Desire

A soul rises up, restless
with shuddering desire for God
and desire for the salvation of souls.

For some while now, she has given
herself to the arduous pursuit
of virtue, and has become

accustomed to dwelling
in the vertiginous cell
of self-knowledge, desiring

still better to know God's
nearness, having seen
how love is borne

upon knowledge. Thus,
loving, she will pursue Truth,
and drape herself in His beauty.

∽ A Revelation

My true servants—even if their love
remains imperfect—seek Me
for love's sake alone, rather than
the consolations and delights
they find in Me. Though I reward
every smallest kindness, the measure
of that prize remains the recipient's love.

For that reason, I send the sweet
consolation of prayer now one way,
and now another. It is not My will
that the soul receive her consolation
foolishly, nor greedily, paying more
attention to the gift than to its source.

Most of all, I desire that she attend
to the charitable love in which the gift
is given, to suspect how little
she deserves it—thereby glimpsing love's
immensity and thereby avoiding
the error of taking pleasure
without attending to its loving Cause.

⮞ Inebriated Soul in Love

Then that soul, even as one drunk,
appeared to be beside herself,
parted from her bodily senses due
to union with her Creator.
She raised her spiritual eyes, her *nous*,
and gazed into eternal Truth.

As she now came to know the Truth,
she knew herself to be in love with it.

She said aloud: O high
eternal Goodness, O my God!
What am I—the wretched one—to You,
O soaring, everlasting Father,
that You have shown Your truth to me?
that You have shown the snares
the evil one has set? the snares my own
selfish heart lays out for me?
What moved in You to do such things for us?

Love alone, love unreturned, You have poured out
Your love without my answering love!
O fire of love Who burns me!

Saint Catherine of Genoa
(1447–1510)

A member of the noble family of Fieschi, she sought to enter the convent at the age of thirteen, but was denied due to her youth. At sixteen, she married a suitor who turned out to be an unfaithful and violent man. After ten years of unhappy marriage, she received mystical revelations, which are expressed in her two works: the Dialogues of the Soul and Body, *and the* Treatise on Purgatory. *She spent the remainder of her life in tending the sick, especially during the plague that ravaged Genoa in 1497 and 1501.*

∾ Agapi

Even in her lucent flesh, the giddy soul was met
by the God's igniting love, a passion that
consumed her, making limpid every element,
so that on that troubled day she was to pass
from this life, she might wake unhindered, blinking,
in His Presence, and fully there. But even here, dwelling
in His love, she swooned, and the fraught circumstance
of souls in purgatory—where they are being freed
of all impediment—became known to her, and she also
knew joy in union with the God in His loving crucible,
and look! also rejoicing now the souls whose lives
are element by element made fuller there.

∞ In the Crucible

These souls cannot so much as think,
I am here, and justly for my sin, nor
can they stammer, *Would that I
had never sinned in such a way.*
They recall neither the good
nor the evil in their pasts, nor the faults
of others. For such is their joy
in God's good will, their joy in His
good pleasure, that they retain
no concern for themselves, but dwell
only in the joy of God's compassion
and decree, and in the joy of seeing
Him do just as He will. They see
only His goodness, His mercy
to them. In a twinkling, perhaps,
they had glimpsed the cause of their suffering
at the moment they departed earthly life.
After that, such small knowledge
disappeared, eclipsed by the immensity
of Love alone. There is no joy save the joy
of paradise to compare with that joy
of souls being made whole again.

∽ *Provisional Matters*

I see my soul torn
from all spiritual things
that could give it solace
and joy. And my soul, suddenly,
has little taste for past pursuits
of intellect, or will, or memory,
and in no manner tends
more to one thing than
another. Quite still,
and in a state of siege, the *me*
within me finds itself
gradually stripped of all
that in spiritual or bodily form
gave it comfort. And once
the last of them has been
lifted clean away, the soul,
comprehending that they were
at best remedial, turns
away from them completely.

Saint Nil Sorsky
(† 1508)

Before becoming a monk, Saint Nil Sorsky worked as a book copier. Later in life, he took monastic vows. He and his brotherhood would later become known as the Volga startsy and the saint would become their leader. At one point, he journeyed to the Holy Land, to Constantinople, and to Mount Athos, learning the mystical practice of Hesychasm and poring over patristic literature. Upon his return to Russia he founded a cloister on the Sora River, where he and his disciples pursued lives of noetic prayer.

∽ What Afflictions Avail

If not for sufferings, the unknowable
    Providence of God would not be apprehended
        as acting on the crowd. And we would be
unable to approach God with boldness,
    unable to learn the Spirit's wisdom
        or be assured of divine love in our souls.

Prior to sufferings, the poor man prays
    as to a stranger; but if, out of love, he struggles,
        soon he observes a stirring change.
Before this, he held God as a taskmaster,
    but now becomes God's true friend.

⁓ The Gift of Tears

Like the tears of an infant, weeping
even as it laughs (see how he rejoices!
spiritually expressing his deepest joy
even there on his tear-streaming face!), such
is how the gift arrives, springing forth
without any effort of our own. May
our Lord grant each of us such tears!

For us beginners in prayer, frail and
inexperienced, these tears become
our greatest consolation; and note,
as this consolation by grace is given us,
the tears themselves increase, and so on.

With tears, the struggle with the enemy
turns easier, the temptations are quenched,
and the *nous* is fed—delighting in prayer—
by a surfeit of nourishing food.

⁓ Sayings

No oars are needed if the sails are full,
but if the ship is stopped in dead-calm,
one must set to rowing.

When, finally in contemplation, you find yourself
in living union with the God, do not allow
your mind to wander in distraction, for those
who turn idly away from this remembrance
of God commit a spiritual adultery.

Saint Isaac explains that prayer is like a seed,
and ecstatic prayer is like the harvest.

Whenever the soul is drawn by prayer's activity,
it is drawn to what is divine, and becomes like God
by this unspeakable union.

As Saint Paul writes, *Eye has not seen,*
nor has ear heard, nor have so much as entered
into the heart of man those things the God
has prepared for those who love Him.

Saint Simeon elaborates: *In such a state,*
I have no desire to leave my cell, but wish
only to descend deeply as in an earthen pit,
that there, removed from all else, I may gaze
upon my eternal Master, my Creator.

Saint Isaac agrees: *When the blindness*
of the passions are lifted from the noetic eye,
and a person leans into this glory, then
he ascends, draped in awe.

Saint John of the Cross
(1542–1591)

Born at Fontiveros, a village near Ávila, the saint is revered for assisting Saint Teresa of Avila in restructuring the Carmelite order. He is best known for his mystical—if intermittently philosophical—writings. His poetry and his meditations on the development of the soul—especially his Dark Night of the Soul—*are prized as the most beautiful of mystical literature in Spanish.*

∽ Dark Night

Of a dark night, kindled in love
and aching with desire—happy chance!—
I went out without being observed,
my household being at rest.

In darkness and confident, I laid hold
of the hidden ladder, and disguised
—happy chance!—by darkness,
my household being at rest.

In that delirious night, in secret,
when no one stirred to see me, I moved
sightless without light or guide,
save that which burned in my heart.

Heartlight guided me more surely
than the light of glaring day to the place
where He—yes I knew!—was awaiting me
in a place where no other soul appeared.

O night that led me, O night more comely
than the dawn, O night that drew together
Beloved and lover—the lover transformed
in the Beloved's embrace!

Upon my flowery breast,
kept wholly for Himself alone,
there He slept as I caressed Him,
while the swooning cedars made a breeze.

The breeze blew from the turret
as I parted His thick locks; with His
gentle hand He hurt my neck
and made all my wits to be suspended.

I stayed put, lost in a swoon;
I lay my face upon the Belovéd's breast.
All things came to a stop, and I forsook every thought,
releasing my burdens among the lilies.

∾ Love's Living Flame

1. O living flame of love
that hurts my soul with tenderness
to its deepest center! As You
no longer press with undue weight, but are
now consummate! If it be Your will,
tear the veil obscuring our encounter!

2. O sweet searing,
O delighting wound!
O tender hand! O delicate touch
that tastes of eternal life
and pays every ransom!
In entering death You turned that death to life.

3. O flames of fire!
in whose flickering splendors
the deep cave of sentience languished
long confused by blindness,
you now give forth, so strangely and so perfectly,
both heat and light to the Beloved.

4. How tenderly and lovingly
You rouse my heart,
where in secret You abide alone;
and in Your sweet breath,
filled with good and glory,
how sweetly You increase
my heart with love.

⌒ Ecstatic Stanzas

I leaned into unknowing,
and there I remained unknowing,
surpassing all that can be known.

1. I leaned into unknowing,
and when I saw myself arrive
without a clue to where I was,
I came to apprehend immensities;
I will not dare to speak what I felt,
for I was held, unknowing,
surpassing all that can be known.

2. That perfect apprehension
was a calm and a holiness
held with no mediation
in utter solitude;
this seemed such a pure hiddenness
that I stood stammering,
surpassing all that can be known.

3. Thus overcome,
absorbed and withdrawn,
my senses were insensate,
torn free of all their powers,
and my spirit was given
understanding without understanding,
surpassing all that can be known.

4. The one who finds his way here
severs from himself the hindered self,
and all things he carried to this place
now appear worthless.
His understanding soars
so that he bides in unknowing,
surpassing all that can be known.

5. The higher he ascends
the less he comprehends,
because the cloud is dark
that lit the night with its flame;
whoever discovers this
remains forever in unknowing
surpassing all that can be known.

6. This knowledge in unknowing
so overwhelms
that the disputations of the world's
wise men can never overcome it.
Their knowledge cannot approach
the understanding of not understanding,
surpassing all that can be known.

7. This subtle, supreme apprehension
is so lofty that no power of man,
no learning, can grasp it.
The one who masters himself
will, with this apprehension
of unknowing, forever proceed.

8. If you should desire
to hear of it, listen now: this highest
apprehension bides
in the very uncreated energies of God,
and this is a work of his mercy,
to leave you without understanding, yet
surpassing all that can be known.

Saint Nicodemos of the Holy Mountain
(1749–1809)

An ascetic and erudite monk on Mount Athos, Saint Nicodemus is best known for having compiled The Philokalia, *the quintessential guide to the prayer of the heart. In his monastic pilgrimage, Nicodemus aspired toward perfection, seeking a spiritual father in order to exercise the great virtue of obedience, hoping that through obedience he might attain greater spiritual accomplishment in prayer, in humility and contemplation of God.*

✑ *Noetic Vision*

When finally the mind
staggers to its home
within the heart, it must
not lie there languishing.
Having discovered the *nous*—
that is, the subtle
reasoning of the heart

through which we may
partake intuitively of truth—
let the mind say nothing else
besides *Lord Jesus Christ,*
Son of God, have mercy on me.

Then note: It is not enough
to do this carelessly,
but necessary to overcome
the distractions of the soul,
so that the prayer is uttered
with all your will and power and love.
I'll say it clearly: Teach
your inner understanding
to say only this Jesus Prayer,
and train your mind
to pay attention only
to these words, leaning in
to their expansive meaning,
free of all distracting forms
or shapes or your imagining
any other thing, even
if it is a good thing, for God
exceeds all such imaginings,
and if you would be joined
to Him through prayer,
you must also move
beyond all mere perceptions.
That is where your union
will occur.

⌒ The Mind's Home within the Heart

All things find refreshing
calm and peace when they
have found their center.
As the lowly snail finds rest
within its crusty shell,
as an octopus tucked within
its still chamber, as the fox
within its den, the bird
folded into its nest, so the man
whose mind—now stuttering
in distraction—seeks his latent,
natural capacity to rest, finds
stillness when it enters the heart,
the subtle and the inner man.

As the animals, when troubled
or raised to fear, run directly
to their dens to be protected,
so also the mind of man, when
assaulted by evil thought
or any manner of internal
or external threat, must know
to rush to the heart and cry there,
My Jesus, help me! My Jesus,
be my sole salvation!

✑ A Plea

A third time, then, I beg of you
to keep *Jesus* as the sweet, sole
contemplation of your heart.
Let *Jesus* be the chief
preoccupation of your tongue.
Let *Jesus* be the honorable
shape and substance
of your mind. In short,
let *Jesus* be your very breath,
and never tire of calling out
His name, which performs
and manifests the union
and the unifying agency
of both the God and man.

Saint Thérèse of Lisieux
(1873–1897)

Known and beloved as the "Little Flower," Saint Thérèse died when she was 24, having lived as a cloistered Carmelite for less than ten years. Her life was private and her sole work was prayer; the only record we have of that pursuit, released after her death, is a summarized edition of her private journal, published as The Story of a Soul.

∿ *Eternal Canticle*

Even far from heaven, I still can sing.
Your promised one—hear her, Lord!—still sings,
giving her everything to Love's eternal canticle.
She feels Your quick flight to her in response—
Your Holy Spirit's fire from above.

Matchless Beauty and my Love! I am amazed
that You give Yourself entire, that give Yourself
entirely to me. Here, take my heart,
take *all* my yearning heart! Make of my life
one single act of love, and all expressed to You!

Will You infuse my worthlessness with worth?
Will You take my squalor as home?
Love occasions ever greater love—appalling grace!
In helpless adoration, Lord, I press to reach Your side.

Love that enflames, enter and inflame me now!
Do You hear? I cry out to You! Come now to do Your will!

Love compels me, desiring that I might ever be
Engulfed and lost in You, Fierce Crucible divine!

Whatever pain is borne for You turns suddenly to joy.
Regardless of all else, my love flies to You as a cooing dove!
Heavenly Everything, Lush and Loving Fullness, Immeasurable
Sweetness, may my soul receive You here, even as above.

Heavenly Everything, Lush and Loving Fullness, Immeasurable
Sweetness, everything You are and all You do is Love!

ᴈ Attend

Notice! Jesus stands just before you,
waiting in the tabernacle shaped
for you—shaped precisely for you!
He burns with great desire
to enter into your heart.

Ignore the yammering demon
telling you "not so!" Laugh in his pinched face
and turn without fear to receive
the Jesus of quiet calm and utmost love.

Partake of His Mysteries often,
often as you can, for in Them you find
your sole, entire remedy, assuming—
of course—you would be cured. Jesus has not
impressed this hunger in your heart for nothing.

This gentle Guest of our souls
knows our every ache and misery.
He enters, desiring to find a tent, a bower
prepared for His arrival within us,
and that is all, all He asks of us.

⌒ *The Flower*

The earth is stilled, snowbound,
        and roundabout, a bitter hoarfrost clings.
Winter and his henchmen
        hold all and everything in a grip of pain.

But look! amid that frozen waste
        a single Flower rises from the earth
new arrived from heaven's fatherland,
        where springtime eternally gives birth.

Sister! Approach the Rose of the Nativity
        and there among the modest grasses bide.
As the humblest of the petals,
        await the King and be His bride!

∿ The Holy Face

And when, Lord Jesus, I chance to glimpse
   Your Holy Face it sets me once again
upon the way, both my Path and my sole Beckoning.
   Your brow becomes my Paradise on earth,
Your gaze reveals—as radiant, lucent gems—Your eyes
   still glistening with tears, and through my own
fresh tears I smile to You, and find Your grief
   has suddenly eclipsed my own small pain.
I would delight to live precisely thus,
   utterly effaced, if it would then
console Your Heart's longsuffering.
   This subtle beauty is sweetly shown to all
who live thus unattached to mundane care.
   I would abandon all to dwell with You.

In this way Your Face becomes my home,
   the radiance of my days, my realm
and sunlit land, where—all my life—
   I raise a murmur, uttering Your praise. As lilies
carpeting the valley floor, You fill
   the air with mystic scent, which I breathe in
whenever I grow faint; it gives sufficient
   foretaste of the peace that is to come.
Your Visage bearing this immortal grace
   is like most holy myrrh to me. It is my
music and my instrument, my rest
   and resting place, my all and everything—Your Face.

Therefore my sole desire is Your Face, and so
        I wish nothing more than this: that as I
contemplate Your Holy Mystery, I grow
        more fully to resemble You. O Jesus, press
upon me now some lasting trace
        of Your sweet, humble, ever-patient Face.

Epilogue

⟋ *The Words*

So it is with the Torah,
    which discloses her innermost secrets
        only to the one who bears love for her.
She knows that whoever is wise,
    day after day, trembles in love
        at the gate of her dwelling.

What does she, but reveal
    her face to him, offering a sign of love,
        then withdraws again to her secret cove.
He alone will hear her call,
    and is by that beckoning drawn to her
        with his whole heart, entire soul, full being.

In just this way, the Torah,
    in a moment, opening, discloses herself
        in love to her lover, and so arouses him.

—*from* The Zohar, *c. 1280*

ABOUT PARACLETE PRESS

Who We Are

Paraclete Press is a publisher of books, recordings, and DVDs on Christian spirituality. Our publishing represents a full expression of Christian belief and practice—from Catholic to Evangelical, from Protestant to Orthodox.

We are the publishing arm of the Community of Jesus, an ecumenical monastic community in the Benedictine tradition. As such, we are uniquely positioned in the marketplace without connection to a large corporation and with informal relationships to many branches and denominations of faith.

What We Are Doing

Books | Paraclete publishes books that show the richness and depth of what it means to be Christian. Although Benedictine spirituality is at the heart of all that we do, we publish books that reflect the Christian experience across many cultures, time periods, and houses of worship. We publish books that nourish the vibrant life of the church and its people—books about spiritual practice, formation, history, ideas, and customs.

We have several different series, including the best-selling Paraclete Essentials and Paraclete Giants series of classic texts in contemporary English; Voices from the Monastery—men and women monastics writing about living a spiritual life today; award-winning poetry; best-selling gift books for children on the occasions of baptism and first communion; and the Active Prayer Series that brings creativity and liveliness to any life of prayer.

Recordings | From Gregorian chant to contemporary American choral works, our music recordings celebrate sacred choral music through the centuries. Paraclete distributes the recordings of the internationally acclaimed choir Gloriæ Dei Cantores, praised for their "rapt and fathomless spiritual intensity" by *American Record Guide*, and the Gloriæ Dei Cantores Schola, which specializes in the study and performance of Gregorian chant. Paraclete is also the exclusive North American distributor of the recordings of the Monastic Choir of St. Peter's Abbey in Solesmes, France, long considered to be a leading authority on Gregorian chant.

Videos | Our videos offer spiritual help, healing, and biblical guidance for life issues: grief and loss, marriage, forgiveness, anger management, facing death, and spiritual formation.

Learn more about us at our website:
www.paracletepress.com, or
call us toll-free at 1-800-451-5006.

SCAN
TO
READ
MORE

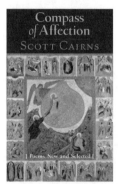